Living Sacrifice

Living Sacrifice
The Cross as a Way of Life

Robert Gelinas

Published in association with the literary agency of Wolgemuth & Associates, Inc.

ISBN: 0692373160
ISBN-13: 978-0692373163

To Frank Embree

Contents

The Call of the Cross

The Way of the Cross

Choosing the Cross

Preview — *Finding the Groove*

The Call of the Cross

To this you were called, because Christ suffered for you,
leaving you an example,
that you should follow in his steps.
1 Peter 2:21

Chapter 1

A Strange Invitation

Strange Fruit

He stands stripped bare, arms restrained at the wrists. His legs are lacerated on all sides; long, deep grooves cover his torso and lumps of flesh are missing. Only a slight grimace of his mouth hints at the immeasurable torture he has endured. Illegally arrested and unjustly convicted, they whipped him without mercy. Surrounded by a jeering, mocking crowd, he has no friend in sight. Hundreds have gathered to watch, as he is moments away from hanging on a tree, dying a humiliating death reserved for those without citizenship.

His name was Frank Embree.

Without Sanctuary: Lynching Photography in America[1] is a pictorial history of lynching in America, and it was there that I first saw the three pictures of Frank Embree taken in 1899. Each stomach-turning page of the book brings home the tragic reality of this form of execution, which was commonplace in America. Lynching was expedited "justice" served through torture and vigilantism. Most trace its origins back to the 1700s and Colonel Charles Lynch who bore the ironic title of Justice of the Peace. He often held illegal trials and, upon inevitable guilty sentences, would tie the "convicted" to a tree to be flogged. By the late 1800s, "Lynch Mob" was a part of the American vocabulary and used to describe the horrific practice of confiscating a "criminal" from the local jail or kidnapping him from his home in front of his family. Then, without proper trial, the mob would disgrace, whip with barbed wire, torture, emasculate and hang their often-innocent victim.

Frank Embree was one of thousands of Americans—mostly black—who were victims of lynching. They were hung from trees with their bodies mutilated, lacerated, burned and/or riddled with bullets. It was a community event often led by unmasked—yet usually never punished— perpetrators. Pictures show men and women gathered

---

[1] James Allan, Hilton Als, John Lewis, Leon F. Litwack, (New Mexico: Twin Palms Publishers, 2008).

by the thousands to witness these hangings. Even children were recruited to assist in the grotesque gatherings. It became tradition to cut off parts of the victim's body as memorabilia. People even posed for pictures with the corpse; the photographs , which were sometimes sold as postcards, depict surreal scenes of men with rifles, people cheering and children playing with the body suspended above their heads—a necktie party.

The pictures of Frank Embree show a young man of only nineteen years of age standing tall in the back of a buggy; the look in his eyes reveal centuries of his people's search for dignity. After a rope was slipped over his head, a final picture shows him as he dangles with crooked neck, eyes still open, a loin-cloth covering—his only article of clothing.

Bronx schoolteacher Abel Meeropol saw one of these pictures and put pen to paper, writing the disturbing poem, *Strange Fruit*. He then convinced jazz singer Billie Holiday to lend her distinct voice to the haunting tale of . . .

Southern trees that bear strange fruit,—
Blood on the leaves and blood at the roots . . .
The bulging eyes and the twisted mouth . . .
The sudden smell of burning flesh . . .
Here is a strange and bitter crop,—[2]

When Holiday performed the song in concert, her audiences didn't know how to respond. She sang beautifully, but the lyrics were disconcerting; were you supposed to sit in silence or applaud? Holiday felt the dilemma equally and never quite knew what song to sing after *Strange Fruit*. She eventually moved it to the end of her performances and made it the last song of the night.

After all, how do you follow strange fruit?

That's a difficult question, isn't it? How do you follow strange fruit?

Perhaps you've never thought of it this way before, but, as followers of Christ, we have wrestled with this question for centuries. How do we follow strange—unnatural—fruit? After seeing a lynch victim, one author wrote, "He had been stripped of all his clothing with what appeared to be a loin cloth positioned below his hip. The figure was eerily reminiscent of the image of Christ being crucified on the cross."[3] This is a comparison that many have seen, Ida B. Wells being one of them. A former slave and orphaned by a yellow fever epidemic that took her parents, she was left with five siblings to raise on her own. In the 1890s Ida

---

[2] Excerpts from poem
[3] Paula J. Giddings, *Ida: A Sword Among Lions* (New York: Amistad, 2008), 275.

launched a campaign against lynching after a friend of hers died at the hands of a lynch mob. Putting her skills as a writer to use, she chronicled the practice for a larger audience. Her campaign against lynching often made reference to the crucifixion of Jesus, for the comparisons between the two forms of execution are obvious. As one author wrote, "The loveliest lynching was our Lord."[4]

Like Frank Embree and countless others, Jesus was kidnapped in the dead of night by a blood-bent mob, put through mock trials and found guilty without proper procedure. His execution on the cross was a scandal—the ultimate in degradation. While the Romans didn't invent crucifixion, they perfected it through practice. Untold thousands of victims hung to their deaths, with humiliation and torture as the chief goal in the excruciating process reserved for non-citizens of the empire.

The cross was a scandal—the ultimate of disgrace—a curse. Jesus was stripped bare and hung in dishonor. Impaled with unfathomable brutality and unable to swat a fly, His nail-inflamed nerves pulsated. He hung there, mocked, lips chapped, tongue swollen, family dishonored.

He was strange fruit.

---

[4] Paula Giddings in *Ida: A Sword Among Lions* has a chapter by this title.

Core to Christianity

Robert Lewis wrote, "We could not make sense of the New Testament in particular, or Christianity in general, without its central figure—Jesus Christ. Christianity is not a philosophy or an ethic, but a person: Christianity is Christ. But neither can we make sense of Christ himself without his cross."[5] Christ was strange fruit indeed as He hung on that cross-formed tree. It was the Apostle Paul who said, "Christ redeemed us from the curse of the law by becoming a curse for us, for it was written: 'Cursed is everyone who is hung on a tree'" (Galatians 3:13). But the question still remains: How do we follow strange fruit?

By becoming strange fruit!

To be a disciple of Christ is to follow Jesus, even to the cross, for the cross is core to knowing Christ. The goal is for us to be able to say, "I have been crucified with Christ and I no longer live, but Christ lives in me" (Galatians 2:20). The Apostle Peter also understood that we are to become strange fruit. Jesus told Peter that He was going to have his arms stretched out and led where he didn't want to go. (see John 21:18). Legend says that he was crucified, literally, upside-down, and still he calls us all to see the cross as a

---

[5] Robert Lewis, *The Glory of Christ* (Chicago: Moody Press, 1997), 291-292.

pattern for our lives:

> To this you were called, because Christ suffered
> for you, leaving you an example, that you should
> follow in his steps. (1 Peter 2:21)

To be a disciple of Christ is to follow Jesus, even to
the cross. The cross is core to knowing Christ.

*God has a singular desire that He is working in every
moment of our lives: That we, too, would become strange fruit.* It
is the destiny that we look forward to, for "we know
that in all things God works for the good of those who
love him, who have been called according to his
purpose. For those whom God foreknew he also
predestined to be conformed into the likeness of his
Son" (Romans 8:28-29). The good that God is doing
in all things is the molding and shaping of us into the
image of His only begotten—crucified—Son. When
you and I devote our lives to God, He uses every
moment to conform us to Christ—that we would *live
and love like Jesus.* That we would speak, listen and act as
He would because "we, who with unveiled faces all
reflect the Lord's glory, are being transformed into his
likeness with ever-increasing glory" (2 Corinthians
3:18).

This idea is developed even further in Ephesians
where we are called to "be imitators of God, therefore,

as dearly loved children and live a life of love, just as Christ loved us and gave himself up for us as a fragrant offering and sacrifice to God" (Ephesians 5:1). Our imitation of God is to extend to loving "just as Christ loved us" on the cross. Paul was so compelled by this call of God that he took it on as his deep desire, saying, "I want to know Christ and the power of his resurrection and the fellowship of sharing in his sufferings, becoming like him in his death" (Philippians 3:10). Wow, to answer the call to become like Christ in His death. What would it take? What would it look like to pursue the death of Christ with our lives? In all circumstances the ultimate question is, "God, how does this make me more like the crucified Christ?"

Not Just for Jesus

Sometimes in my devotional moments I take a piece of aluminum foil and conform it tightly to a crucifix. It is a tactile prayer of pressing and squeezing that brings into reality what God is trying to do in our lives. Namely, conforming our words and wallets, lips and life until it is lived out of the cross. The crucifixion is not *just* about what Jesus did but what we are *becoming*. This doesn't sit well for those of us who have been conformed into the image of this world (see Romans 12:1-2). We are doers and so "being conformed"—

someone else doing something to us—grates against us. Yet we are called to offer ourselves as living sacrifices for God to do with us as He desires. We must survey the wondrous cross and come to grips with its call. *We must see that Jesus, in His death, was actually showing us how to live.* For by our fruit—our strange fruit—we are to be known.

The apostle Paul said, "I resolved to know nothing . . . except Jesus Christ and him crucified" (I Corinthians 2:2). This is the journey: To know Christ by knowing His cross. The scriptures call us not to just know *about* the cross but to know the cross, intimately, to embrace it *as a way of life.*

People of the cross desire to know Christ and His suffering. But knowing is wrapped up in doing. When it comes to the cross the goal is not just an intellectual understanding of what Jesus accomplished in His crucifixion. Rather, we must pursue the cursed death of Jesus until we see it as the life we must choose if we desire to know Christ. It's about knowledge gained through experience. The result of knowing the cross of Christ is that it becomes a way of life.

Rich Mullins, in his song *The Breaks,* reminded us of this when he sang these words . . .

It's the sea that makes the sailor,
It's the land that shapes the sea

I don't know where I am going or where I'll some day be.
It's the wood that makes the carpenter,
It's the very tools of his trade.
It's love that makes the lover and
the cross that makes a saint.

The cross is an invitation. Have you responded to its call?

My RSVP

When I survey the wondrous cross, I am horrified. Tattered and torn skin . . . blood-matted hair . . . pain-induced quivers . . . the death of God. A man so battered and betrayed that words fail.

Selah[6]

When I survey the wondrous cross, its beauty startles me. The life. The love. The compassion of the death of God. It, no, *He* summons me to feast upon that which I gaze. For some unresolved reason I accept the offer.

Selah

When I survey the wondrous cross, I am haunted.

For my soul knows . . .

my inmost being bows in contrition . . .

---

[6] Selah is a term found throughout the book of Psalms. While its definition is not known for sure, many believe that it means to pause and reflect.

compunction convicts.

> My hands, my thoughts, my
> eyes betray the reason for the
> death of God.

Selah

When I survey the wondrous cross, I am mystified. I search for its meaning, for its understanding, for the "whys" of what I see. What was God doing on the cross? There are so many answers. The more doctrine digested, the more elusive, yet simultaneously adjacent, the death of God becomes.

Peter, why couldn't you have kept its meaning to yourself? "To this you were called, because Christ suffered for you, leaving you an *example*, that you should *follow in his steps*" (1 Peter 2:21, emphasis added). Why must you involve us? Why must you summon me? As if we want to. As if I am willing to follow the example of Christ and His cross.

The cross is an example, an intricate design, on which we lay the transparent parchment of our lives and sketch our feeble outlines.

The cross is to be followed, like tracks in the snow. We step high and sink in deep to the openings made by The One who has gone before.

Excruciare. Latin for "out of the cross." Excruciating People: those who live life out of the cross. *Christians: those who have accepted the invitation to live an excruciating life.* The cross is a way of life—an ethos—mores, not just morals. The cross is a culture for pain-absorbing, price-paying, peace-making, love-wielding, cup-drinking people.

When I survey the wondrous cross, I am terrified. For what I see and know demands my soul, my life, my all.

Selah

Chapter 2

The Heart of the Matter

A Well-Worn Path

Frances Xavier Cabrini founded the Missionary Sisters of the Sacred Heart of Jesus with the simple aspiration of spreading devotion to the heart of Christ through acts of mercy. During her time on earth she established "sixty-seven hospitals, orphanages and schools—one for each year of her life."[7] In the foothills just west of Denver is the Mother Cabrini Shrine. For more than two decades, I have visited this place multiple times a year because it reminds me that *the cross is a way of life.*

You see, Mother Cabrini would often walk with her

[7] "History of Mother Cabrini Shrine," Mother Cabrini Shrine, accessed May 14, 2014, http://www.mothercabrinishrine.org/.

adopted orphan children to the highest point of the mountain. In 1954, a stairway of prayer was constructed along this well-worn path. The three hundred seventy-three steps to the top lead you to a twenty-two-foot tall statue of Jesus, standing upon an eleven-foot pedestal facing east. His right hand extends palm up toward the millions of people who reside below in the Mile High City's metro area. With His left hand, He pulls His robe aside, revealing to the world His heart, encircled by a crown of thorns. I've always found this image intriguing. *We talk so much about inviting Jesus into our hearts, but what if the invitation is to enter His?* Is the objective for us to get Jesus into our lives or for us to enter into His? After all, it is "*in him* [that] all things hold together" (Colossians 1:17, emphasis added).

The climb up to the statue takes you past fourteen crosses that mark the Way of the Cross (also known as The Stations of the Cross). Attached to each wooden cross is a stone mosaic depicting an episode in Christ's Passion. Benches are placed in front of each station so you can sit and consider the road of suffering that our Savior followed. Among the scenes portrayed are Christ's condemnation by Herod, Jesus' taking up of His cross, His struggle to carry the cross, His humiliation in being stripped naked and His body nailed upon the tree.

On one of my first dates with my then future wife, I took her to this sacred place. At dusk we climbed hand-in-hand along the way of the cross. At the top we watched the sun set behind the Continental Divide to the west, and we prayed as we looked out over our city lights with the statue of Christ watching over us. Though our relationship was young, our hearts knew that this was right and that God was calling us to walk the way of the cross together.

Eventually, the chill of the evening chased us from the overlook, sending us back down the steps to the warmth of the car. When we reached the exit of the shrine parking lot, however, we were stunned to find the gate closed. We were locked in!

There was a light on in the nearby stone house, so we drove to it and knocked. One of the Sisters opened the door and sternly informed us that the mountain closes at sundown. She then put on her boots with her habit, hopped in a nearby 4 x 4 truck and unlocked the gate.

Today, Barbara and I smile every time we drive through that same gate in our fifteen-passenger van, filled with our six children and their friends. As we stand in a circle, holding hands and praying the Lord's Prayer before we climb to the top with our children, we remember how it all began. Although, I wonder how Mother Cabrini did it! I've discovered it's not easy to consider the way of the cross while trying to keep track of wondering and wandering children. Along the ascent they vacillate between complaints and questions. Life out of the cross has to be able to permeate all of our activities, the serious and the mundane. It is not a distraction; it is the attraction.

Once we reach the top, the inevitable item for discussion is the lightening rod sticking out of the top of Jesus' head. A bolt of lightning damaged the statue during a thunderstorm and the rod was added during the reconstruction. When it happened, I gathered our children together and told them with all seriousness, "You're not going to believe this: Jesus was struck by lightning, and He lost an elbow, hand and foot!" Shocked expressions looked up at me. They rolled their eyes when I told them I was talking about the statue at the Mother Cabrini Shrine.

I continued and asked, "But how is Jesus going to love our city without an arm and hand? How is He going to give it a hug?" My eldest daughter exclaimed, "Dad, that's not *really* Jesus, and, anyway, *we* are Jesus' arms!" I guess they *were* paying attention as we walked the way of the cross.

Compelled

Simon was forced to carry the cross while trying to keep track of his children (see Mark 15:21). He and his sons, Alexander and Rufus, were in Jerusalem for the Passover when a Roman soldier forced this nameless face in the crowd onto the stage of history. It's my guess that Simon resisted—wouldn't you? "Sir, I can't help, I'm just visiting with my sons." But the soldier, seeing a falling and failing Jesus, just wanted someone to get the job done. Simon had no choice as he picked up the crude device of torture, already wet with blood and sweat, and began to follow this battered man. I'm sure at first he just tried to keep an eye on his sons in the crowd, but I hope as time passed, he also allowed the eyes of his heart to take in this strange figure he was following.

What did he think as he saw Christ's cut and bleeding body? Did he lump Him in with the other two criminals?

I wonder (no, I hope) that something happened to Simon that changed his mandate into a labor of love for our savior. Perhaps Jesus looked him in the eyes, and—in that moment—Simon realized he was not just seeing but being seen. Or maybe Jesus spoke to him,—it may have been a simple "thank you,"—for words spoken by Jesus, no matter how brief, could have penetrated his defenses. Perhaps he went from having to carry the cross to wanting to, from being compelled to finding it compelling.

When he rejoined his sons, did he see their names

in new light? After all, Alexander means "man-defender" and Rufus, "red." Their father had just carried the cross of the defender of all mankind and even had the red bloodstains of Jesus on his shirt.

Were they captured by the tragic drama? Were they still around the city on Sunday? Did they hear about and feel the rumblings of the resurrection (literally! See Matthew 28:2)? Mark doesn't tell us what happened to Simon and his sons, and this could be because his original readers already knew the answer. When Luke writes of the church at Antioch he mentions a Simeon (another name for Simon) called Niger. Then during the riot at Ephesus there is a man called upon to give a defense for the people named Alexander (remember his name means "defender of man"). And later when Paul sends his letter to Rome, he mentions Rufus (and his mother) in the closing chapter (see Acts 13:1; 19:33 and Romans 16:13).

Whatever the case, what we hope for Simon should be what we desire for ourselves: that we don't feel compelled to walk the way of the cross but that we find it compelling. Only Christ could actually bear the cross (with a little help from Simon), but we are to carry the cross (with a lot of help from Jesus) as we follow "in his steps." Our journey is strangely similar to his.

Perhaps it's the simplicity of the Mother Cabrini

Shrine that keeps drawing me back. When I'm there the call of Christ makes sense. For instance, the Stairway of Prayer at the shrine begins and ends with the crucifixion. At the bottom there is a tall crucifix that you encounter before embarking on the journey. For me it serves as a reminder that the cross existed in the mind of God before Christ bore it that sorrowful day. After climbing to the top and seeing the magnificent view of the resurrected Christ inviting the world into His heart, you eventually have to make your way down, and the last thing you see on the journey is the same image of Christ on the cross again. I have sat beneath that crucifix for countless hours, letting its meaning sink in: *Walking with Jesus begins and ends with the cross—the cross is a way of life.*

Sometimes we can think that the cross was something for Jesus to experience, and we vicariously enter in for the purpose of understanding what was done for us. But the cross was not just for Jesus. It's for us too. We are people of the cross, and even though twenty centuries separate us from it, we must always keep it near. Like jazz does the blues.

Blue Notes

The Blues were born out of pain and suffering and soaked in the rawness of life that doesn't always go the way we want. The blues gave birth to jazz, and jazz never forgets this. In jazz, the blue notes are the ones that play with pain until tragedy turns into comedy. Blue notes linger simultaneously in between the major and minor. They are flat, slightly dissonant, yet expectant. Good jazz music always remembers that it is rooted in the blues and, in one way or another, pays tribute. In the same way that jazz can't leave the blues behind, neither can we have a Christian life without the cross.

The temptation is to bypass the cross while still gaining the benefits. Remember when Jesus fasted forty days in the desert and the tempter saw an opportunity to derail His mission (see Matthew 4:1-11)? One of the devil's tactics was directly related to the cross. He led Jesus to the top of a mountain and showed Him the kingdoms of the world. It was a way of laying before Christ all that He had come for and then offering Him a deal. If Jesus would just bow in worship of him, then he would hand over all that for which Jesus came. In essence he said to Jesus, "I'll give you the crown without the cross." If Jesus would have accepted, He could have avoided the flogging and the nails, the rejection and the suffering. Instead, Jesus chose the way of the cross and responded, "Away from me Satan! For it is written: 'Worship the Lord your God, and serve him only'" (Matthew 4:10). In the eyes of Jesus, true worship in the kingdom of God had to include submission to the cross.

Embracing the cross as a way of life is not easy. It is nothing short of accepting an invitation to an excruciating life, and when do, we become a song that allows the blue notes to be heard. This will require that we ask and answer two questions:

What was Jesus doing on the cross?

How does the death of Christ teach us how to live?

But we must be careful how we ask.

Cross-Examen

It is easy to ask questions of the scriptures—and ultimately God—in a way that is wholly inappropriate. Job learned this lesson. He was a man who lived a righteous life. He prayed, studied the scriptures, worshipped God sacrificially and even made a "covenant with his eyes not to look lustfully at a woman" (Job 31:1). His faith was more than the private practice of piety—it was heartfelt and real. As he described himself in his own words: "I was eyes to the blind and feet to the lame. I was a father to the needy; I took up the case of the stranger" (Job 29:15-16).

And then one day his life fell apart and he sat singing the blues upon a pile of ashes. Little did he know he was part of a cosmic wager between God and The Accuser. What he did know is that he had lost everything—wife, children and business—with no explanation why. He spent the following days asking questions and listening to friends pontificate upon his situation.

Now, there is nothing wrong with asking questions. Jesus invited and entertained them all the time. However, there is a difference between asking questions of God and questioning God. It is the latter that Job slipped into as he took on the tone of a lawyer cross-examining God as a defendant in a courtroom. When Job crossed that line, God quickly reminded him about his place in creation.

How we ask our questions matters. Jesuit Christians practice what they call the Prayer of Examen. It is a simple form of prayer that seeks to develop receptiveness to the call of God for the purpose of a response. The idea is to slow down daily and posture oneself before God's gaze with a listening heart.

As I learned at Mother Cabrini's the way of the cross is meant to be a prayer. When considering the suffering of our savior, we must do so with our heart on its knees. The goal is not to examine but examen. Examine is a scientific term. Examen is devotional. There are times when we need to examine the scriptures for the purpose of gleaning the facts, but we should do so humbly and quickly. Otherwise, we risk placing ourselves in the role of questioner. In a similar way, I believe that when we approach the cross we should spend the bulk of our time not as the cross-examiner, rather we should prayerfully allow the cross to examen our lives.

Thankfully for us, those who have walked the way of the cross before us have garnered from the scriptures the classical answers to *what* God was doing on the cross. For centuries, the church and its theologians have studied the scriptures and formulated the concepts in answer to the big question: If Jesus was the sinless Son of God, then *why* in the world was He hanging on the cross? (Or more simply put, What was Christ *doing* on the cross?) The answers are self-evident in the scriptures, and they are the bedrock of Christian faith. They take five basic themes: Substitution, Redemption, Reconciliation, Christos Victor and Submission. Over the centuries, scholars have given these different, but not competing, answers based upon the times in which they lived and the passages of scripture emphasized.

- Substitution: Jesus was absorbing our pain by taking our place.
- Redemption: Jesus was paying the price for our freedom.
- Reconciliation: Jesus was making peace between God and His creation.
- Christus Victor: Jesus was securing victory over sin, darkness and death.

- Submission: Jesus was submitting to the will of His father.

I wish I could say that the hard work has been done for us, but it hasn't. Knowing what Jesus was doing on the cross is the easier part. Answering the second question, How did Jesus in His death show us how to live? will require that we allow ourselves to be cross-examined.

To want Jesus is to want the cross. To follow Christ is to embrace the wood beams, the nails and the pain gladly and with thoughtful intent. Hebrews points the way, "Let us fix our eyes on Jesus, the author and perfecter of our faith, who for the joy set before him endured the cross, scorning its shame, and sat down at the right hand of the throne of God" (Hebrews 12:1-2). Prayerfully approaching the cross as a way of life allows us to not just read the Bible but also allow it to read us.

The cross is a way of living, not just believing. It is more than a proposition, it is praxis and devotion, a way of life, and a culture in and of itself. Ultimately, we are not to examine the cross more than we are to be examined by it. What matters most is not what we say about the cross of Christ, but what His cross says about us.

In the next section of the book, each chapter will examine one of the classic answers to, "What was

Jesus doing on the cross?" and then show how that eternal truth leads us understanding, "How does the death of Jesus show us how to live? As we continue, may the Father, Son and Holy Spirit guide us to see more clearly how Jesus in His death was calling us to a new way of living life by losing it. May God grant us hearts willing to respond to the call of living sacrifice.

The Ways of the Cross

Then he said to them all: "Whoever wants to be my disciple must deny themselves and take up their cross daily and follow me."
Luke 9:23

Chapter 3

Pain-Absorbing

Substitution

God knew that we would have a hard time with this concept. As children it was fine and necessary that people did things for us, but now that we're grown up we need to be responsible for ourselves. We can eat, get dressed and pay our bills on our own. It's an admission of weakness to have someone do something for us, especially when we caused the trouble in the first place. So God knew we weren't going to easily accept the whole idea of one taking the place of another, especially when the One is God himself. Yet, core to understanding the cross of Christ is grappling with the *self-substitution of God.* That's why God spent so much time imbedding the concept in the history of his people.

This imbedding process began with Adam and Eve. God gave them the garden for their enjoyment, including all but one of the trees. They (like us) chose the only one outside the will of their creator. Separation and enmity ensued. God in His mysterious sovereignty already knew that He was going to take our place, wedged between His holiness and love. But, for the moment, God allowed Adam to watch the death of an animal he named, trading its skin for his feeble fig leaves.

Substitution: One can take the place of another.

Then came the Passover lamb. As God passed over the people on that fateful night, the death of a lamb without spot or blemish served as a substitute for the firstborn son's life. The foreshadowing was unmistakable when God instructed them to apply the blood on the door frame—top to bottom, right to left—the blood formed a cross. But just in case we would miss the connection, the crucifixion happened on Passover. "For Christ, our Passover lamb, has been sacrificed" (1 Corinthians 5:7).

Upon seeing Jesus, John the Baptist shouted twice, "Look, the Lamb of God, who takes away the sin of the world!" (John 1:29,36). He could have been alluding to Jesus being the Passover lamb, but most likely he was making a broader statement about the whole sacrificial system. For centuries God's people picked out unblemished lambs, goats and pigeons when they sinned. Worshipping God consisted of bringing a substitute for sins committed and seeing that substitute lose its life on behalf of the sinner.

Abraham had a front row seat to God's redemptive, substitution-oriented drama. Following the command of God, he marched with such amazing faith, calculating that somehow God was going to resuscitate his son, whom he would sacrifice. Oh, the helplessness Abraham must have felt as his son asked, "Daddy, where's the sacrifice?" How did he deflect Isaac's questions? How did he ignore the terror of his son when he realized what was about to happen? How relieved and thankful Abraham must have been to see the ram (the substitute for his son) in the thicket and the angel coming to save him from the mystifying request of God (see Genesis 22).

Why would God ask His servant do such a thing? How could He possibly ask a father to sacrifice his son? This side of the cross we know that God could and would identify with the extreme agony Abraham experienced, for God knows exactly what it feels like to sacrifice His one and only Son. The episode with Abraham was just another scene in God's unfolding revelation of what would become reality.

When Jesus arrived on this planet, He knew that He

was going to suffer in the place of His creation. For centuries Christ watched us sin in subtle and salacious fashion, all the while knowing that He would eventually be the one to take the penalty for each act of rebellion. The Holy Spirit looked over Isaiah's shoulder as he put pen to papyrus and wrote:

> Surely he took up *our* infirmities
>   and carried *our* sorrows,
> yet we considered him stricken by God,
>   smitten by him, and afflicted.
> But he was pierced for our transgressions,
>   he was crushed for *our* iniquities;
> the punishment that brought us peace was
>   upon him,
>   and by his wounds we are healed.
> We all, like sheep, have gone astray,
>   each of us has turned to his own way;
> and the LORD has laid on him the iniquity of
>   us all.[8]

Sometimes when I read those words, I replace the word "our" with "my." When I do, I sink to my knees in bitter regret for all that I have done. If I had sinned less, would Jesus have suffered less? I don't know, but

---

[8] Isaiah 53:4-6, emphasis added

I'm sorry. We are sorry. Forgive us.

For Me

There is an old hymn that helps us connect in times like these.

Wounded for me,

>Wounded. What an understatement!

The soldier's clenched fist that Christ didn't even see, that's just one way you were wounded for me.

Wounded for me,

>Tied to a post and flogged. At least thirty and nine times, the leather straps slapped his skin, the lead balls pounded and tenderized His muscles, the sharp bones imbedded and ripped His back into ribbons of flesh. Blood flowed freely from Jesus' wounds.

>Purple robe ripped. Crown of thorns smashed.

There on the cross He was wounded for me;

>As I picture Jesus hanging on the cross and I imagine His wounds on my body.

>GOD died for me?

>God DIED for me?

>God died FOR me?

>God died for ME!

>God was the ram in the thicket, my substitute. My infirmities (sickness, anxiety, calamity),

sorrows (griefs), and transgressions (revolts) were lifted up with Christ upon the cross. Jesus took the nails for our part in the rebellion, that ancient uprising in the garden.

*Gone my transgressions, and now I am free, All because Jesus was wounded for me.*9

I'm struck by how God is both holy (unable to be in the presence of sin) and loving (desiring us poor sinners) at the same time. How He blended the two together and decided to absorb the pain for me. Somewhere in eternity past, His righteous anger burned and His unending love poured forth to quench; and Jesus, in chorus, was sent and to live and die a pain-absorbing life.

Wounded—substituted—for me.

For You

Peter says that understanding substitution is the basis for seeing the cross as a way of life. "To this you were called, because Christ suffered *for you*, leaving you an example, that you should follow in his steps" (1 Peter 2:21, emphasis added). Can it be? Peter suggests that what Jesus did in His death is what you are to do with your life. The death of Jesus is to be your path. When Christ took your place on the cross, He absorbed your

---

9 *Wounded For Me by William Ovens and Gladys Roberts*

pain, and now the church, as a cross-formed community, is to be a pain-absorbing people.

Jesus said we are salt. Salt seasons, but that requires that it will also be crushed between teeth. It slows down decay, which requires that it be in intimate contact with that which is decomposing—the pain of the world. Seeing the cross as a way of life requires massive amounts of courage. It is not natural to seek out burdens meant for others and to take them on as our own. Taking the place of another goes against our innate survival instinct.

I know a life of substitution is possible for me because I can remember times when I took someone's place when it came to positive, beneficial things. There have been times in my life when there were accolades due someone else, yet I substituted myself and enjoyed them. At times I've taken credit for that which I did not do. Even for that which God did. We all have done this. God does something through us and then we take the glory, *His* glory. So what's clear is that we can take someone else's benefits, but now, as cross-cultural people, we must resolve to take someone else's burden.

Peter doesn't mean that we can take the place of others in the exact same way that Christ did. Only Jesus, the sinless Son, could die on the cross for our sins, satisfying once and for all the righteous wrath of

God. No, what Peter is saying is that we purposefully seek out those in this world who are in pain and then live in their presence in such a way that relief results. Their lives get better; our lives get worse— substitution.

Cuckoo

I've heard heroic stories of people living pain-absorbing lives.

When a prisoner escaped from the Nazi death camp known as Auschwitz, the Nazis chose ten people to die for the escapee's offense. Franciszek Gajowniczek, one of the ten, began to plead for his life, hoping that his captors would spare him because he was a husband and father. They showed no mercy. Also present that day, hearing the desperate man's pleas, was a man who understood substitution. He was prisoner #16670, a Polish priest by the name of Father Maximilian Kolbe. He asked if he could take the man's place. The switch was made. Father Kolbe was the last of the ten to die on August 14, 1941.

Or I think of Florence Nightingale, the mother of modern nursing. Born to the well-to-do, she gave her life to serving the poor and sick because she heard the voice of God at the age of nineteen. Knowing a God who left comfort to be with us, she made the same decision and began serving the poor, diseased and sick in hospitals and infirmaries. She lost much because of her calling—the respect of her parents, her marriage; she even had a mental breakdown. Her life became less so that the lives of others might be more.

The Society of Jesus (The Jesuits) is a monastic movement that gives themselves to friendship with Jesus and a willingness to do anything for the kingdom of God. There are stories of these Christ-followers going to prisons and actually seeking to exchange themselves for those incarcerated. The condemned goes free as they serve *in their place.*

But Peter seems to say that the heroic should be normal for people of the cross. Like the foster or adoptive parent who takes another's child into their home. As the substitute, stand-in, parent, they must be prepared to absorb much. Adoption is one parent taking the place of another and providing love and care. It is being there for first steps and first-aid. It is stepping in and taking on the obligations that the original parent could not, for whatever reason, provide. But it also means that, in some cases, you absorb the pain of another. Some children have seen their lives shattered. It's hard for them to comprehend the adult world that crumbled and left them without home, friends and stability. Sometimes they do understand and are rightfully enraged. Either way, it is the adoptive parent who, as a way of life, absorbs the pain due another. When their child lashes out with words of frustration and actions of anger, trying to cause harm, it's the new, substitute parent's job to absorb what is meant for another . . . in the name of Jesus . . . as Jesus did for us.

Reed Warblers unknowingly serve as parental substitutes. They are birds whose eggs resemble that of the Cuckoo Bird. What Reed Warblers don't know is that when they are away from the nest, the Cuckoo sneaks in and lays its eggs. When the Warbler returns, it doesn't recognize that it has been volunteered to be a substitute parent! It now must find enough food for its young and the Cuckoo's as well. While the Cuckoo is out having fun, the Reed Warbler is spending sleepless nights trying to figure out how it's going to pay for braces and college tuition for all of these kids!

That's my fear. It's hard enough to volunteer to live a pain-absorbing life, but there are a whole lot of Cuckoos out there too!

Black and Blue

The Holy Spirit of God must cultivate in us the strange fruit of burden bearing. It is God who helps us know the difference between a backpack and a boulder. Paul wrote, "Carry each other's burdens" (Galatians 6:2a). By that he meant that if we see someone carrying a load too heavy for them, it is our calling to let their burden become our burden. The image in the original language is that of a huge boulder. No one should have to go through life trying to carry (or push) a huge rock around, even if they were the ones who took the hammer and chisel of bad choices and cut it out of the quarry with their own hands. But then Paul wrote, "for each of you should carry your own load" (Galatians 6:5). Here, in the original language, we have the image of a backpack. Everyone should carry their own backpack, but if we spot someone whose load has turned into a burden (boulder) then we are to take our free shoulder and lift a corner of their rock. The weight we carry will become more, but theirs will feel lighter.

Tim Keller observed that, "real love requires personal exchange."[10] The kind of love that the cross shows us is the kind that trades joy for sorrow and life for death. As Keller wrote, "In the real world of relationships, it is impossible to love people with a problem or a need without in some sense sharing or even changing places with them. All real life-changing love involves some form of this kind of exchange."[11] This is especially true when we are in relationship with people who are in pain. "To bring them up

---

[10]Timothy Keller, *The Reason For God: Belief in an Age of Skepticism* (Dutton: New York, 2008), 193.
[11] Ibid., 193.

emotionally you must be willing to be drained
emotionally . . . All life-changing love toward people
with serious needs is a substitutional sacrifice. If you
become personally involved with them, in some way,
their weaknesses flow toward you as your strengths
flow toward them."[12] The cross calls us to love like
this, to love as we have been loved.

Bishop John Rucyahana, serving amidst the
aftermath of the Rwandan genocide ,said, "If a woman
who was raped and beaten and forced to watch as her
husband and children were tortured and killed before
her very eyes can forgive in the name of Jesus Christ
those who did such a horrible thing, then any victim
anywhere, can forgive in the same way."[13] Forgiveness
is a rather strange fruit of the cross.

To forgive is to experience pain twice. First, there is
the pain of the offense, and then there is the pain of
forgiving. The pain of letting go of the need to be paid
back for the pain caused to us. Jesus felt this double-
pain as well. First He experienced the broken heart of
having His creation defiantly choose the path apart
from Him, and then—in order to wipe the slate
clean—He endured the second pain of the cross. In

[12] Keller, *The Reason for God,* 194.
[13] John Rucyahana with James Riordan, *The Bishop of Rwanda:
Finding Forgiveness Amidst a pile of Bones* (Thomas Nelson:
Nashville, 2007), 221.

Christ we see that to forgive is a pain-absorbing way of life.

This is what makes forgiveness so difficult. It requires that we take on more pain in the midst of pain. Jesus didn't wait for the pain of the cross to pass before offering forgiveness. He didn't speak the words, "Father, forgive them for they don't know what they are doing," after the resurrection but during the crucifixion (Luke 23:34). Again Pastor Keller says it so well:

> Forgiveness means refusing to make them pay for what they did. However, to refrain from lashing out at someone when you want to do so with all your being is agony. It is a form of suffering. You not only suffer the original loss of happiness, reputation, and opportunity, but now you forgo the consolation of inflicting the same on them. You are absorbing the debt, taking the cost of it completely on yourself instead of taking it out on the other person. It hurts terribly. Many people would say it feels like a kind of death.[14]

Forgiveness means absorbing the debt of sin yourself.[15] As [Dietrich] Bonhoeffer says:

---

[14] Keller, *The Reason For God,* 188-89.

everyone who forgives someone bears the other's sins. On the cross we see God doing visibly and cosmically what every human being must do to forgive someone, though on an infinitely greater scale.[16]

Reginald Denny was the man who was pulled from his truck during the riots of South Central Los Angeles and brutally beaten. The world watched as video cameras captured two men beating him with bottle and brick until he lay unconscious, his face caved in.

When it came time for the trial, cameras were present again as Denny approached the mothers of the perpetrators and told them that he forgave them.

After observing the event, one commentator stated, "Well you know, Denny did suffer some brain damage."

Forgiveness. So painful and contrary to our nature that it can lead observers to wonder if the one granting forgiveness is in his right mind. The foolishness of the cross (see 1 Corinthians 1:22-24).

It was Louis Armstrong who sang the sorrowful song, "Black and Blue." He was such a joyful man with

---

[15] Ibid., 192.
[16] Ibid., 192.

a one-of-a-kind contagious smile, but not when he sang this song. In it, he tried to sort through the haunting question, "What did I do to be so black and blue?" Jesus could have asked the same question. What did Jesus do? Nothing. Absolutely nothing.

Christ asks the same of us.

Chapter 4

Price-Paying

Ransom

Jesus stated his mission clearly: "For the Son of Man did not come to be served, but to serve, and to give his life as a ransom for many" (Mark 10:45). Not only was Jesus absorbing our pain on the cross, he was also paying a ransom. When an army conquered its foe and took them captive, they would then send word to the relatives of the POWs, offering their beloved fathers and sons back for a price. Or, in the ancient world, when someone was indebted to another to the point that they belonged to that person, they became a slave until they worked off their obligation, or until someone else paid the price.

Ransom: The price paid for freedom.

The cross is layered with meaning. Not only did Christ taking our place (substitution), but that place-taking counted as currency (ransom). He was capital offered in payment for our freedom. But why would God give us our freedom again? Isn't that like taking a drunk back to the bar after you've picked him up from the local detox center? Exercising our freedom is what led to our troubles. At first, freedom seems like a good thing, but we have not used it well.

Adam and Eve had freedom before the fall. They walked with the Lord God in the cool of Eden as He explained the platypus and mosquitoes. God gave them the freedom to eat of any tree in the garden (except one). They enjoyed perfect relationship with the Creator and perfect union with each other. Yet they were drawn to the one tree they could not have. In their freedom they walked by the Tree of Life and traded its potential for the knowledge of good and evil. Why did knowledge seem better than life? Why did knowing what God knows seem better than being with the God who knows?

We can't just blame Eve for partaking of the forbidden fruit because Adam was there too. RIGHT THERE! The scriptures say, "she took some and ate it. She also gave some to her husband, who *was with her*, and he ate it" (Genesis 3:6, emphasis added). The whole time Eve was being deceived, her husband stood by in hushed stillness, watching her.[17] Adam said nothing? John Eldredge insightfully points out that "there was a moment in Eden when Eve was fallen and Adam was not: she had eaten, but he yet had a choice . . . Adam chose Eve over God."[18] Wow. Adam sat there with the fruit in hand and pondered life with Eve in a fallen state versus life with God untarnished. In his freedom he eventually concluded that life apart from God seemed more desirable.

We make the same insane choice. Our souls are all too familiar with the knowledge of good and evil. The fruit of that tree promises so much satisfaction; though, when the feast is finished, emptiness is all we have to show for responding to its enticement. Our minds swirl with the wonder of the ease at which we have succumbed.

We know that "every good and perfect gift comes from above" (James 1:17), but how is it good for God to give us freedom again? We have a track record of using God's gifts against Him. God gave us metal in the ground, trees in the forests and skill in our hands. With that skill we mined the metal and chopped down

---

[17] Larry Crabb has explored this in depth in his book, *The Silence of Adam* (Zondervan, 1998).

[18] John Eldredge, *Wild at Heart: Discovering the Secret of a Man's Soul* (Nelson: Nashville, 2000), 116.

the trees. But we didn't stop there. We took those gifts and formed a cross and fashioned the nails, and when God sent His Son, we crucified Him with the very gifts He provided.[19] Then God, with compassion beyond comprehension, takes our horrible use of freedom against His Son and uses it for our good—for our freedom. Pascal was so right—love has reason that reason cannot reason; love has understanding that understanding cannot understand!

It's hard to comprehend that Jesus came to set us free when we are self-incarcerated because of the wrongful use of our God-given freedom. We sit in our sin-created dungeons, and in the darkness, we long for the "life that is light . . . the true light that gives light to everyone" (John 1:4,9). Yet we know that God came to that which was His own, and we did not receive Him, for we "love darkness more than light" (John 3:19). In Christ we accept the offer of freedom because it means our release from this present darkness, but how are we so different than Adam and Eve? Won't we wound God again? That seems to be a risk He readily takes.

To fully experience God as our redeemer, we have to face something about ourselves—we are not free.

[19] Paraphrase of Donald Grey Barnhouse, "Epistle to the Romans," Part 37 (Philadelphia: The Bible Study Hour, 1952), 1841.

Apart from God and His kingdom, even our best intentions end up binding us.

Unearned Suffering

Job longed for God as his redeemer. He was such a godly and righteous man. So much so that he even sacrificed for the sins that his children might have committed (see Job 1:4-5). One day he lost everything—livelihood, wealth, workers and every one of his children. Yet, as the day came to a close, he praised God with his pain-numbed heart. He didn't even have time to bury his children when the sores started to show up on his skin and his wife recommended that he curse God to expedite the end of his miserable existence. Then he had to endure the parade of finger-pointing friends who were accusing him of secret sin that must have invited the judgment of God. It was all too much to bear, so he desired two things: to die and meet God face-to-face.

I wish I could ask Job, "How did you know? When you spoke those words, were you delirious from the pain, or did you actually understand what your utterance meant?" Some say all he hoped for was a blood relative that would set the record straight after he died, but he seems to be looking for more than just someone who would correct history. He was longing for a Redeemer, a price-payer, and no mere relative could accomplish this after he was dead. Job's words only make sense in retrospect, in light of Christ, the cross and His resurrection. Somehow Job foresaw the resurrection: "I know that my redeemer lives, and that in the end he will stand upon the earth. And after my skin has been destroyed, yet in my flesh I will see God; I myself will see him with my own eyes—I, and not another. How my heart yearns within me!" (Job 19:25-27).

Job longed for God to not only enter his pain but for God to give it meaning. Is there anything worse than meaningless suffering? It's one thing to experience pain and know why it's happening. At least there is hope that if you figure out the problem then relief is around the corner. Martin Luther King, Jr. pointed out, however, that "unearned suffering is redemptive."[20] That is, if we suffer for something we did not do, at least we know it can make the world a better place and there is purpose in our pain. But Jesus took it a step further, and His blood rescues even our earned sorrows for the kingdom.

Sermon in Our Blood

Maybe that's why Jesus came when He did. He could have chosen any place and time in history to arrive

---

[20] See Martin Luther King, Jr.'s "I have a Dream" speech.

incarnate and carry out His price-paying mission. If Jesus had arrived in the United States anytime in the last two hundred years, He still could have accomplished the goal. He still could have been sentenced to die, but it would have been different. Capital punishment (which is an interesting phrase in light of price-paying) would have been carried out by hanging, electrocution or lethal injections. While all of these methods would have been effective in ending His life, they would have been lacking in a necessary way: the shedding of blood. The torture leading up to and the actual crucifixion spilled so much blood. And as we know from the scriptures, life is in the blood (see Leviticus 17:14).

This truth is programmed into the very workings of our bodies. I like what Dr. Richard Swenson says about life being in the blood; it "is not only good theology but also good biology."[21] Each day our blood literally is our life, as red blood cells circulate through the more than sixty thousand miles of blood vessels (approximately two and a half times around the equator!) bringing life in the form of oxygen. Jesus, You were like us in that Your body produced over two million red blood cells every minute. Your red blood

---

[21] Richard A. Swenson, *More than Meets the Eye: Fascinating Glimpses of God's Power and Design,* (NavPress: Colorado Springs, 2000), 25.

cells were so plentiful that Dr. Swenson wonders, "if God paused when deciding to create red blood cells . . . realizing that His Son would die by shedding them. How much blood did Christ actually shed? . . . without a doubt, He shed at least one red blood cell for every human who ever lived. Mathematically He would have accomplished that in His first few drops. And a drop—even a single cell—of such divine blood is sufficient to pay the price of our ransom."[22]

It's as if God left a witness to his redemption in our very veins. If red blood cells were born to bring life, white blood cells and platelets were born to bring life through their death. When infection enters our bodies or we cut our fingers with a knife, they die so that we might live as they step forward to aid the immune or clotting process. The gospel in our own blood!

God, through his Holy Spirit, guides us, too, toward a price-paying life. Just like Hosea. God persuaded him to marry a prostitute by the name of Gomer. After some time and three children, it became clear to Hosea that though he was faithful, his wife was not. Even worse, he was probably not the biological father of his three children. Gomer left him yet used his generous gifts to provide for her new life with her lovers. Somehow, she ended up a slave, in

---

[22] Ibid., 26.

chains and on the auction block for the highest bidder. I wonder what the Sweet Spirit of God whispered in Hosea's ear to convince him to do what he did. How did God sway him to go to the auction that day and redeem his wayward wife? What an embarrassingly surreal moment that must have been for him as he stood in the crowd. Everyone knew the story and must have thought that he came to see Gomer get what she deserved. But then, as she stood in all her shame, the sale began. Hosea outbid everyone, paying the price for her freedom—freedom she could use to break his heart again.

Spent

Whatever words God used to woo this heartbroken man to such an act of mercy, let us now—as people of the cross—invite Him to whisper those words to our souls, as well, so that we might live life out of the cross. May God grant us willing wallets and open schedules, that we might be predisposed to pay the price for other people's freedom. May God give us keen eyes to see the chains that harness our friends and merciful hearts as we live freely amongst incarcerated people.

I think of former naval officer Jim McCloskey who, after earning a degree from Princeton Theological Seminary, gave himself to serving those on death row—more specifically, the wrongfully accused. In the United States it is now common to hear the story of someone who, after serving years in prison, was released, having been found innocent. Since 1989, approximately two hundred people (overwhelmingly minority), in over thirty states have been exonerated of the crimes they were convicted of, largely due to advances in DNA testing. I praise God for cross-cultural servants such as Jim McCloskey who go searching for the incarcerated in our midst, seeking their redemption. Jesus was wrongfully accused and unjustly convicted too. That's why I love the name of McCloskey's endeavor: Centurion Ministries,[23] for there was a Roman centurion "who stood there in front of Jesus, heard His cry and saw how He died he said, 'Surely this man was the Son of God!'" (Mark 15:39).

There is a prayer that price-paying people need to become comfortable with if we are going to live redemptively: Spend me. The prophet Isaiah more than hinted at this when he spoke God's words:

> Is this not the fasting I have chosen: to loose
> the chains of injustice and untie the cords of
> the yoke, to set the oppressed free and break

---

[23] For more information, visit www.centurionministries.org.

every yoke? Is it not to share your food with the hungry and to provide the poor wanderer with shelter—when you see the naked, to clothe him, and not to turn away from your own flesh and blood? . . . If you do away with the yoke of oppression . . . and if you *spend* yourselves on behalf of the hungry and satisfy the needs of the oppressed then your light will rise in the darkness, and your night will become like the noonday. The Lord will guide you always.[24]

A life that redeems people from their prisons of poverty, hunger and oppression is a life that is spent. Like currency—capital—like the spare change that is thrown into the jar on the dresser at the end of the day. Like Jesus spent His precious blood on that dreadful day. "Spend me," must be our prayer.

Spend me . . .

. . . on that person imprisoned by their past. That person at school who can't outrun their story, for, wherever they go, it has already arrived. Help us to see how we can spend our time for their freedom, as we sit with them and learn new stories of what God is doing in their life, and then generously tell those tales

---

[24] Isaiah 58:6-7,9-11, emphasis added

until they overshadow the old narrative.

Spend me . . .

. . . on behalf of the girls at Marembe House. Pregnant teens (often not by choice) who are abandoned by their families find themselves trapped. Be with those who care for them and their precious little ones with physical and emotional medicine and nourishment, giving them a hope and a future.[25]

Spend me . . .

. . . on those caught up in religion. "Do this! Don't do that!" They genuinely think that is what it means to know God. They are so caught up in trying to please God that they can't glimpse the gift of grace.

Spend me . . .

. . . on places. Help us to see old run-down movie theatres as houses of worship[26] and brothels in Cambodia as orphanages for HIV/AIDS children.[27]

***

Jesus told us there is something that precedes a price-paying life: servant hood. As He said, "For the

---

[25] For more information, visit www.mirembehouse.com.

[26] The church I pastor, Colorado Community Church, currently meets in a renovated movie theatre next to a liquor store.

[27] For more information, visit www.cambodianoutreachproject.org.

Son of Man did not come to be served, but to serve, and to give his life as a ransom for many" (Mark 10:45). Christ came to serve. He was "The" Servant, but anybody can be "a" servant. That's why we love the story of Ruth. It's the story of pain redeemed, and it reminds us of how two widowed women, trapped at the bottom of society, found a "kinsman-redeemer" who served them, loved them (ultimately married one of them!) and spent his life in practical ways on behalf of them. In the end, he and Ruth found love, and their little story of redemption gave way to "The" story of redemption, as their offspring eventually produced the ultimate "Kinsman-Redeemer"—Jesus.

Where would we be without people who served us redemptively? I remember one time in junior high Sunday school. We were all sitting in a circle praying (supposedly). Staring at me from across the circle sat Jeffrey. And while our teacher was trying to lead us in prayer, I was threatening my classmate. I didn't like him looking at me. so I glared at him. Then I showed him a clenched fist. He continued, so I dove across the circle. Over we went in his chair, and, with my finger pointed in his face, I told him to stop looking at me, or else! My Sunday school teacher didn't throw me out. No, redemption isn't about throwing away; it's about spending oneself in service until the person has a new purpose. There are no guarantees. The person might use their second-chance freedom to return to old ways.

That's just a chance we have to take.

Chapter 5
Peace-Making

Reconciliation

I thank God for Mrs. Genn, my Sunday school teacher who constantly taught us about the cross.

I remember the time she drew a vertical line on the chalkboard and talked about how Jesus came so that we could have a relationship with God. Then she drew a horizontal line and said that Jesus also came so that we can be right with each other. Pointing at the intersecting lines that formed a cross, she said, "Because of the cross, we can be in right relationship with God *and* each other."

Another time Mrs. Genn wrote the word "atone" on the board and explained that it meant "to make things right." Then she said that if we had a hard time remembering that, all we had to do is make two words out of the one. Below the word "atone," she wrote, "at one."

Reconciliation is another essential aspect of the cross. On the cross Christ made it possible for us to be "at one" with God and "at one" with fellow human beings. "For God was pleased to have all his fullness dwell in him, and through him to *reconcile to himself all things*, whether things on earth or things in heaven, by making peace through his blood, shed on the cross" (Colossians 1:19-20, emphasis added).

Irreconcilable Differences

Sometimes I forget just how bad things really are and that this world is not even close to what it was meant to be. Christ hung on the cross for the purpose of peace and reconciliation, but that assumes we understand that relationships have gone bad. In the garden—when things were right—Adam and Eve experienced perfect relationship with God, each other and the rest of creation.

When sin entered the world, the first thing to go was relationship with God. When relationship with God is right, then peace flows to the rest of our relationships, so the emergence of sin had devastating results on every other relationship. Likewise, any attempt to have good relationships with others without first drawing near to God is futile. The first eleven chapters of the Bible demonstrate this vividly.

Genesis shows us that Adam and Eve were naked and unashamed (see Genesis 2:25). They lived fully exposed (naked), without feeling self-conscious about what others might see (unashamed)—now that's peace. This is supposed to be the norm in the marriage relationship. God designed us, male and female, for intimacy. That is, to be known and to fully know without pretense or fear. This is exactly what Adam and Eve had. How beautiful it must have been. No need to show off or pretend. No need to worry about misspeaking or having to perform for the sake of love.

Adam never did anything to land himself in the doghouse. He didn't have to go through the garden picking flowers to form a bouquet of apology to bring home to his beloved. Eve never wished that she encouraged her husband more and criticized less. Adam never had to sleep on the couch or watch Eve leave the house in a huff. He never wondered when his baby was going to come home. There was no need to leave because life together was home. Life together with God is the ultimate definition of home.

All of that changed when they felt the urge to sew fig leaves together. For the first time, when they heard the voice of their Creator calling, they didn't run to Him. They crouched in shame, staring at each other in fear. There they realized that not only was there something between them and God, but also something had crept in between the two that were supposed to be one—irreconcilable differences.

Adam, then "scapegoated" his wife.[28] She was the very bone of his bone and flesh of his flesh, yet he took the first opportunity he could to lay blame outside of himself when he said, "The woman you put here with me—she gave me some fruit from the tree, and I ate it" (Genesis 3:12). Not only did Adam try and blame Eve, but he insinuated that it was God's fault as well.

When God ushered Eve and Adam out of the garden of no shame into the shadowlands of fear, they had no idea how far the deterioration of relationships would go. Once union with God is compromised, the

---

[28] Little did Adam know that many years later God would turn the scapegoat into an institution to symbolize that He truly will take the blame upon himself. The high priest would lead two goats to the ceremony, and the casting of lots would doom one to death and the other to desertion. After the first goat absorbed the pain of our sin, the other goat suffered a different kind of death. Hands were laid upon it, and sins were confessed. Finally, it was led into the wilderness and released to a life of separation. It's no coincidence that the scapegoat ritual occurred on the Day of Atonement (AT-ONEment) (see Leviticus 16).

male and female bond was only the first to experience the effects of shame and guilt. Next came sibling rivalry.

What hurt God's heart the most? The fact that Cain murdered his brother or even thought. "am I my brother's keeper?" was a legitimate question? (see Genesis 4:8-9). Once that notion is even conceivable as an option, the family can't survive.

Noah and his family co-existed one hundred twenty days in the ark. Any family that has road tripped together recognizes how amazing that is! After that feat, and witnessing the rainbow of God's covenant, they must have felt like they had a bond that could survive anything. Then Noah decided to get drunk and "lay uncovered inside his tent" (Genesis 9:21). When his sons came across his nakedness, at best, they covered Noah's shame. At worst, they somehow disgraced their dad in a way that is not entirely apparent. After Noah sobered, he was incensed and cursed his younger son to slavery (see Genesis 9:18-24). East of Eden family disintegrates (or should it be "dis-integrates"?).

First Things First

As our memory of the Tree of Life faded, we still tried to hold ourselves together. We had a plan: "Come, let us build ourselves a city, with a tower that reaches to the heavens, so that we may make a name for ourselves" (Genesis 11:4). But God thwarted it, for we cannot return to what we had in the garden without first returning to Him. At Babel He gave us a big hint about relationships east of Eden: *Peace with God precedes peace with those around us.* If we are not going to first have peace with Him, then we can't—He won't allow us to—have peace with each other. Yet while He blocked access to the garden and the Tree of Life, access to Him is always a possibility. God sojourns *with us* in the land of fear and shame. So that when we wake up we will find that He is not far away.

As a pastor, I see this all the time. So many are trying to have good relationships with each other without *first* having a good relationship with God. Well-meaning couples, living together before marriage, seek security and some sort of insurance policy against divorce, not recognizing that they need only to invite God in first and then the rest follows. It's a law that God has set in place: *peace with God precedes peace with others; no peace with God, then no peace with others.*

Reconciliation is not the absence of conflict but the presence of peace. Christ desires for us to have whole relationships without shame, but we often settle for so much less. It's not just about argument reduction with a college roommate or co-worker; rather, the cross points the way back to Eden (even though we are a considerable distance from its guarded gates).

Jesus brings a peace that will ultimately extend to all creation; even predator and prey will enjoy each other's company. When I was in South African I saw a man wrestling with tigers. It looked fun as they splashed around in the water together, but the man's darting eyes displayed cautious fear. There was respect and well-founded trepidation about the predator. True peace was noticeably absent.

Jesus is the Prince of Peace not the "Prince of the Lack of Conflict." The day is coming when we will not have to watch our backs at work or see quail fly frantically from us (see Isaiah 9:6 and 11:6-8). We look forward to the day when the whole of creation is soaked in the shalom initiated by Christ's suffering. For now, however, the birds still fly away, squirrels won't allow us to pet them and snakes and spiders still give us pause. Christ stayed on the cross to *atone* so that all might be *at one*.

> For he himself is our peace, who has made the two one and has destroyed the barrier, the dividing wall of hostility, by abolishing in his flesh the law with its commands and regulations. His purpose was to create in himself one new man out of the two, thus making peace, and in one body to reconcile

both of them to God through the cross, by which he put to death their hostility. He came and preached peace to you who were far away and peace to those who were near. For through him we both have access to the Father by one Spirit.

Consequently, you are no longer foreigners and strangers, but fellow citizens with God's people and also members of his household, built on the foundation of the apostles and prophets, with Christ Jesus himself as the chief cornerstone. In him the whole building is joined together and rises to become a holy temple in the Lord. And in him you too are being built together to become a dwelling in which God lives by his Spirit. (Ephesians 2:14-22)

At Babel we united to build a way up and God scattered that effort. On the cross, God came down to bring us together, and—as the cornerstone—now builds us up as a holy tower.

Reconciliation was essential to our Prince of Peace, so much so that Christ knelt on the night that He was betrayed and prayed that we would be *at one* with God and each other, so that the world would know that the

Father sent Him (see John 17:20). Jesus died so that in Him we no longer have to live according to the barriers of society. Not that gender, race and ethnicity disappear, but rather that we live on earth as it is in heaven. In the book of Revelation we gain a beautiful glimpse of the throne room of God, where we see every nation, tribe and tongue *at one* with each other, singing praises (see Revelation 7). When we are right with God, then we can be right with each other.

Advice from an Atheist

Even atheists can see this. Hemant Mehta sold his soul on eBay. The highest bidder, a man with a desire to help churches, purchased him for $504. He in turn asked Mehta to visit a number of churches and write about his experiences as an outsider on the inside.

Mehta offers advice to us church folk on how to reach out to people without faith. Interestingly he sees the implications of the cross when he wrote about the unfulfilled dreams of Dr. King.

> Martin Luther King, Jr. is said to have observed that eleven o'clock Sunday morning was the most segregated hour in America. Based on the research I did for this book, I would say that still holds true. With very few

exceptions, the churches I visited were either black congregations or white ones . . . You want to reach people like me? Then show me the churches where . . . I can see a rainbow of people in the crowd instead of a sea of whiteness or, in another neighborhood, a sea of blackness . . . I'd love to see Christian faith leading to an openness and equality, respect for people no matter their gender or skin color or language or culture. Think about this: atheist gatherings are often a mixture of everyone in society . . . Does it surprise you that secular people are leading the way in accepting others, no matter their individual differences?[29]

Jesus in his death was showing us how to live. That means His calling is our calling. It seems odd to say it this way, but to follow Christ means that we are to have excruciating relationships. That is, relating to each other out of the pattern set forth on the cross. Jesus said that the one who chooses to make peace is blessed (see Matthew 5:9), Peacemaking is an essential part of our job description as those who bear Christ's name. We are to be ministers of reconciliation. If we have been made new, then we seek peace in all areas of

---

[29] Hemant Mehta, *I Sold My Soul on eBay* (Colorado Springs: WaterBrook, 2007), 171.

life (see 2 Corinthians 5:18-19).

Bishop Caldwell knew that something had to be done. As pastor of a predominately black church in Shreveport, Louisiana, he made a startling announcement: he would pay whites to attend!

He was tired of looking out over his congregation of five thousand worshipers and seeing only African-American faces looking back. He was willing to pay whites five dollars an hour to attend Sunday services and ten dollars for a weeknight gathering. He said, "This idea is born of God. God wants a rainbow in his church . . . The most segregated hour in America is Sunday morning at eleven o'clock. The Lord is tired of it, and I'm certainly tired of it . . . this is not right." I've never met him, but I admire him. His approach may be debatable, but his heart is right on track. He looks at the city in which he lives—some 200,000 people divided between black and white—and then considers the cross and God's word and knows that something has to change among the people of God. Most pastors would be happy about five thousand people attending, and yet Bishop Caldwell is not satisfied because he knows that Christ died for so much more. If it meant reaching into his own wallet to bring about your kingdom, that's what he was willing to do.

Passing the Peace

That's why that ancient tradition of the passing of the peace is so important. On the one hand, when we look someone in the eye and say, "Peace," we are making a statement that we want the work of Christ on the cross to flow into our relationships. Additionally, it's a profound, searching question: "Peace? Are we at peace with each other?"

Jesus didn't die to see how many people we could fit into a room on Sunday morning. Yes, He desires that we worship together regardless of hue of skin, but still the goal is deeper: Peace. He desires that we not only share space on Sunday but that we are welcome in each other's homes and we share life together.

The country and people of South Africa have a special place in my heart. In high school I lamented Apartheid (which means separateness). I rejoiced with Mandela's release and election. I hoped when Tutu's Truth and Reconciliation Commission brought perpetrator and victim together, recognizing that "there is no future without forgiveness."

I have always thought that South Africa was one of the thermostats of Africa. This was reaffirmed for me when I boarded a plane in Uganda and struck up a conversation with the man next to me. As a native Ugandan he said, "What Africa needs is 100 more

Mandela's.'" That is, leaders who sacrificially use their power for the common good and then let go of it without bloodshed.

South Africa has a chance to learn from the mistakes of America and do things differently. That's why I was so saddened when I heard in a BBC documentary that the next generation of South Africans don't seem to own the hard-fought battle for reconciliation. Mandela walked out of prison in 1990, but those born since that momentous occasion (they call them "born frees") are at odds with each other. I was distressing to listen to the retelling of race-motivated violence perpetrated by both blacks and whites upon each other.

While Apartheid has officially ended, it still exists in spirit in the church. The BBC interviewer asked a young white man if he had ever dated a black girl. He said, "No, because I'm a Christian." He went on to say that in the same way that he wouldn't date another man because the Bible is against homosexuality, he wouldn't date outside of his race because of what he was told the Scriptures say (see Galatians 2:11-14).

Being born free doesn't mean you are free. Each generation has to rediscover the past and choose to pass the peace.

I think of that old Lone Ranger and Tonto joke about how they were surrounded by a tribe of Native

Americans. The Lone Ranger said to Tonto, "What are we going to do?" Tonto replied, "What do you mean 'we', white man?"

Even the Apostle Peter struggled when it came to societal barriers and relationships. He attended one of the first inter-cultural churches, and, as a Jew, ate with the Gentiles because, in Christ, the walls are removed. But Paul called him out for not "acting in line with the truth of the gospel" (Galatians 2:14). Why? Because he stopped fellowshipping with the Gentiles when some fellow Jews arrived. Paul even accused Peter of hypocrisy because he "began to draw back and separate himself from the Gentiles because he was afraid" (Galatians 2:11-14).

Oh, to truly be *at one* with each other. It would be like that scene in the movie, *Corina, Corina.* There were those two little girls—one black, one white. The little white girl said, "Do you taste like chocolate?" The little black girl replied, "I don't know, do you taste like vanilla?" For the next few moments they proceeded to lick each other's cheeks!

We need the Dove of God to fill us so full that the fear that leads us to hypocrisy has no room in our lives. Perhaps then we would be compelled like Phillip, a Jew with a Greek name, who reached out to an Ethiopian eunuch and became brothers for eternity.

We need the Dove of God to reconcile the wars

that wage within so many of God's children. All too often the reason we fight others is because of the civil war that rages within. So many of us are like John Walker Lindh, the father of the American Taliban. We lack so much peace on the inside that we go searching for it in far off countries only to realize we have become the enemy.

We choose fear because we are trying to avoid pain. We know that love inevitably leads to pain, and so we fear love. If we are going to be God's rainbow people we will have to remember that sacrifice and bloodshed of the innocent ushered in God's covenant.

We must rise out of our pigpens and head back down the road toward home. As we walk, may the Spirit of Peace tell us again about the Father's love and His willingness to forgive. As we return home, may we seek reconciliation with God first.

Crushed

I remember this crush I had in junior high. She was a friend of the girl who lived next door, and we went to school together. I saved my money and bought a small heart-shaped pendant on a flimsy chain. My hopes soared as I wrapped it in its box and labored over the words I wrote in the card.

I envisioned her throwing her arms around my neck

in gratitude as all the boys envied me. I carried her gift around with me for days, but I never mustered the courage to actually talk to her. So I unwrapped the necklace and stuffed it, along with the card, through the thin vent openings of her locker. I watched from afar as she dialed her combination and opened the door to discover my gift. It was so hard to read her reaction as she picked up the chain, grabbed the card and went on to her next class. Now what? All day I avoided her, even as I kept looking for some indication of her feelings. What did she think? Was she writing me a note of adoration too?

I knew which door of the school she exited on her way home, so when the bell rang, I ran out into the adjacent field and laid flat on my stomach, watching. Waiting. Hoping. My heart pounded the ground through my chest as I saw her walk out and make her way toward me. This was it. The moment I'd envisioned. As I stood up, she spotted me and raised her hand as if to wave. I started toward her, but then it became all too clear. She wasn't waving at me. Rather, she was allowing one finger to rise above the rest. She was flipping me off!

It took my heart a while to recover.

God knows that feeling all too well. The prophet Jeremiah chronicles the broken heart of God. He's known as the weeping prophet, and I'm guessing that his tears flowed so easily because it's not easy to glimpse the raw emotions that God expressed to him (see Jeremiah 1-3). God reminisced about His people saying, "I remember the devotion of your youth, how as a bride you loved me" (Jeremiah 2:2). But somewhere things went bad, and God began to wonder, "What fault did your fathers find in me that they strayed so far from me?" and "Has a nation ever changed its gods? . . . But my people have exchanged their Glory for worthless idols" (Jeremiah 2:5,11).

Deeply hurt, God said things about His bride that are hard to read. "See how you behaved in the valley; consider what you have done. You are a swift she-camel running here and there, a wild donkey accustomed to the desert, sniffing the wind in her craving—in her heat who can restrain her?" (Jeremiah 2:23-24). He even called her a lady of the night, saying, "Indeed, on every high hill and under every spreading tree you lay down as a prostitute" (Jeremiah 3:6).

Not only did God share these feelings with Jeremiah, but Ezekiel was a confidant as well (see Ezekiel 16). My Bible calls it an allegory, but the feelings seem real when God told Ezekiel that it was as if He found an unwanted newborn baby girl abandoned in a field. Tenderly God washed off the dried blood and cared for the uncut cord. He swaddled her and provided a safe place for her to learn and grow into a woman. The scene changes as God falls in love with this woman, proposes marriage and makes her a queen. Yet the fairy tale didn't last. God, in His pain, says to her, "you trusted in your beauty and used your fame to become a prostitute. You lavished your favors on anyone who passed by and your beauty became his" (Ezekiel 16:15).

We all have a price. For Judas it was thirty pieces of silver. For others, it's the offer of power and prestige. We have all sought intimacy with God so that we could get houses, cars, jobs, education, ministries and then, with full arms, walked away from God, sending seismic tremors through His heart.

Yet Jesus still slips gifts into our lives. We still find notes in His familiar handwriting with the words, "Come home." We walk outside; He lays in the field, broken heart pounding the ground . . . He courageously stands up.

Our eyes meet. At one.

Chapter 6

Winning By Losing

Christus Victor

I love wrestling with my children. When they were younger, I could take on all six at the same time, but now they're bigger, stronger and smarter. One time they challenged me but I didn't know they had formulated a careful plan. Two took my legs. Two occupied my arms. One ran around, hitting me from all sides, and when I was struggling and befuddled, the last ran and jumped on me, knocking me off balance and flat on my back.

They thought they had victory in their grasp as they all piled on. "Give up," they said. "Give up!" But I didn't. As I lay there, unable to move, I started to whisper, "I win." They couldn't hear me over their celebrations, so I said it again a little louder, "I win." They were beside themselves once they realized what I was saying. One of them leaned down with her nose millimeters from mine and shouted, "What? You can't say you win when you lose!"

Seeing victory in loss. It's as hard as seeing blue in green. It's there, but it's not easy to spot.

When did the war begin?

I'm still kind of fuzzy as to the whys, whens and hows of the hostilities between God and the evil one. I still don't understand why one of God's own shining ones turned on Him. Angels have the capacity to sin like us humans? They are susceptible to pride, arrogance and rebellion? God's word describes the conflict in cosmic dimensions saying, "Michael and his angels fought against the dragon, and the dragon and his angels fought back. But he was not strong enough, and they lost their place in heaven. The great dragon was hurled down—that ancient serpent called the devil, or Satan, who leads the whole world astray. He was hurled to the earth, and his angels with him" (Revelation 12:7-9).

What seems clear is that the war spilled over into this world and now we are involved—deeply involved. The ancient serpent sought Adam and Eve, inquired about Job and salivated at Christ's birth (see Revelation 12). He made every attempt to derail Jesus in the desert and seemed especially concerned with keeping Jesus from the cross. On that high mountain, the devil offered everything, "all the kingdoms of the world and their splendor" (Matthew 4:8). Jesus, though weak in body, was strong in spirit and refused the temptation to take the crown without first taking up the cross. But why did Satan offer? Yes, he wanted Jesus to worship him, but it also seems that he was trying to keep Jesus from something—the cross.

He tried again later. Peter must have been startled when Jesus shouted at him, "Get behind me, Satan!" (Matthew 16:23). Jesus wasn't actually talking to Peter. No, it was to the snake that had been listening as Jesus explained to the disciples the need for the cross (see Matthew 16:21ff). It was the snake's words that Peter spoke, and it was to the snake that Jesus replied.

Jesus' interaction with demons is what gets me most. They talked to Him as if they *already* knew Him. It's as if they were continuing a prior conversation when they said, "'What do you want with us, Jesus of Nazareth? Have you come to destroy us? I know who you are—the Holy One of God!' Jesus commanded, 'Be Quiet!'" (Mark 1:24-25). All of the people were amazed at how the evil spirits obeyed, but what other choice did they have? He was their creator.

They had seen Christ before, hadn't they? It was Jesus who brought them into existence with the same loving care that He did us. Their earliest memories were of Jesus, high and lifted up, with the train of His robe filling the temple with glory. They heard Jesus create us shortly after He created them. They watched as He interacted with humans and bristled as He told them that it was their job to care for us. I'm still amazed when I read their job description: "Are not all angels ministering spirits sent to serve those who will inherit salvation?" (Hebrews 1:14).

Satan seemed to fully understand that Christ came to defeat him and his ways. Ever since God promised Eve that her offspring would crush the serpent's head, he became a student of prophecy. He knew where the Christ would be born and how the Christ would die. He was terrified; after all, he had seen Christ's feet and knew that they would do the job (see Revelation 1:15).

Christ talked about evil spirits and the dragon all the time. For Him, their existence was as real as birds and trees. Jesus taught us to beware of the works of the accuser, the one who seeks to "steal and kill and destroy," but Jesus came that we might have "life" (John 10:10). Jesus, one time in the middle of a conversation about evil spirits, said that if there is a bully, a strong man, then what we need is a stronger man to overpower the bully and tie him up (see Luke 11:14-23). Jesus is that Stronger Man who, right before He went to the cross, said, "Now is the time for judgment on this world; now the prince of this world [Satan] will be driven out" (John 12:31). Jesus directly tied the crushing of the serpent's head to the cross. Victory is what Christ accomplished when He gave his life. But I have to admit it's a strange kind of victory.

Seeing victory in the cross is not readily apparent. It's there, but we have to look hard, like searching for the blue in green. It's our tendency. We live in a culture where winning looks like achievement; therefore, we look for gold medals, contracts and trophies, for press releases, awards and promotions. It hasn't always been this way for us Christians. I'm told that for the first few hundred years, if one were asked, "What was God doing on the cross?" the response would have been, "Christus Victor!"—procuring and proclaiming victory. They would have quoted Colossians where Paul says that the Stronger Man "disarmed the powers and authorities [and] made a public spectacle of them, triumphing over them by the cross" (Colossians 2:15).

Death Disentangled

I want to believe and communicate this about Jesus' cross, but I have to admit that I usually stop short. I tell people about how Jesus absorbed our pain, paid our ransom and made it possible for us to come home and be at peace with God, but I usually don't say that

Christ was decisively conquering the enemy. That He, being the Stronger Man, was "disarming" (stripping bare of weapons and even clothing); "making a public spectacle" (like hanging up a picture in an art gallery) of the dragon and leading him and his cohorts, exposed and naked, through the streets, so that we could see that they can't harm us anymore ("triumphing"). Let us not leave this out of the Good News that we live and proclaim!

When Jesus was nailed to the cross He used one of His last breaths to proclaim, "It is finished" (John 19:30). It was a declaration that the war was over, victory achieved and procured. To the casual observer that day, it looked like God had lost as He dangled on that tree. If we had been there, "victorious" would not have been the first word to come to our minds to describe what was before our eyes. We would have seen a man who was rejected, betrayed, denied, deserted and spread-eagle with vulnerability. But the strange fruit that grew that day was that of victory. The One who was overcome was actually overcoming. The One who looked like the victim was actually the victor. On the cross, Jesus was taking the throne as King—a strangely different kind of king. He had a crown; it was just a crown of thorns. He had a robe; it was soaked in blood. He also had a kingdom, and it is available to all who desire to win. That is, win by losing.

At bare minimum it seems like this should affect how we die. God's Son died on Friday but rose on Sunday. Once and for all He defeated our greatest enemy. Jesus stopped breathing and started decaying, but then all was reversed. God promises this same re-start for every single human being, however we die; whether we are quietly placed in a tomb or have our bodies torn asunder. God will reconstitute our bodies. It's true, whether we are burned at the stake somewhere in church history—our ashes left to drift—or consumed by wild beast in the coliseum—with no evidence of our physical body remaining. God will "unravel" our death.

That's the meaning of the word "destroy": to unravel. In some ways, I'm still trying to get my mind around it.

My friend Dennis knew how to love. He parked his truck in front of his neighbor's house, only to look out later and see a child putting a running garden hose into his truck window, flooding the cab. He ran out and asked the child, "What are you doing?" The child replied, "My Mommy told me to do it."

I'll never forget what Dennis said: "Even in times like that, we're called to be Christians." Daily he sought to unravel wrong with acts of loving kindness toward his neighbor.

When the cross becomes a way of life, evil is

unknotted, injustice is undone and death is disentangled.

I saw my Grandmother lying breathless and cold in the hospital bed. I touched her; she couldn't respond. I talked to her; she couldn't hear me. I asked God to bring her back. His answer, essentially, was "Not yet." Not just her, but all of us.

This should mean that we, as Christians, not only live well but we also die well. I don't know how we are going to die (cancer, car accident, natural causes, etc.) but I know *how* I want to die—I want to die well. If I believe in my life that when I close my eyes I will wake up in God's loving care, then I want to believe that in my death as well.

Co-opted

God must be saddened by how Christ's triumph gets misused. He has led many to see that there is victory in Jesus, but they forget how that victory came about. In the distant past, we Christians sought victory by taking up the sword. We did horrible things in the name of Jesus. Today, so many of us have co-opted the gospel into the American Dream. How many times have we asked God for a car, house or promotion because that is what we believe is our birthright as a result of the victory of the cross? May God give us eyes to see and hearts receptive to the words of Jesus when He said, "I tell you the truth, unless a kernel of wheat falls to the ground and dies, it remains only a single seed. But if it dies, it produces many seeds. The man who loves his life will lose it, while the man who hates his life in this world will keep it for eternal life. Whoever serves me must follow me" (John 12:24-25). We win, but it's the way we win that matters. To follow in the footsteps of the cross means that we believe that death is life and that winning looks like losing. How excruciating.

We want the cross to change not only how we die; we also want to live *life* out of the cross. As we watch the innocent Lamb of God, beaten beyond recognition and fastened to the tree with rough-hewn nails, we see in His death a way of living. We look at the cross and note that it exposes evil for what it really is. And if there is evil, then there is an evil one. But we don't fear him, for Christ put him on display and triumphed through that which looked like tragedy. Let us join Jesus in unraveling the works that continue to rob people of life. But we want to do so in the manner in which Christ did.

Martin Luther King, Jr. understood this when he said, "I choose to identify with the underprivileged. I choose to identify with the poor. I choose to give my life to the hungry. I choose to give my life for those who have been left out of the sunlight of opportunity." If winning looks like losing, then it means we must make a conscious choice to identify with those whom the world deems "losers." Dr. King had an eye for the marginalized of the world and sought to become one with them—to become one of them. He led the civil rights movement to transform the lives of African Americans and change the fabric of American society when it came to race relations. But in the last years of his life, he focused on the poor, regardless of color. King organized The Poor People's Campaign because he made a choice to always identify with those who live in the shadows. The day of his assassination he was in Memphis, marching in solidarity with the garbage workers of that city.

It seems like living with and living for the marginalized should be normal for those who follow the One "who, being in very nature God, did not consider equality with God something to be grasped, but made himself nothing, taking the very nature of a servant, being made in human likeness. And being found in appearances as a man, he humbled himself and became obedient to death—even death on a cross!" (Philippians 2:6-8). That's why the other disciples didn't find it odd when Judas left the Passover meal early. They just "thought Jesus was telling him to buy what was needed for the Feast, or to give something to the poor" (John 13:29).

Zacchaeus climbed the tree because he wanted to

see Jesus, and—as a result—Jesus invited himself over for dinner. People accused Christ of being the "guest of a sinner," but Zacchaeus, used to being overlooked and hated, responded, "Look, Lord! Here and now I give half of my possessions to the poor" (Luke 19:8). He saw what so many of us miss: That if you want to see Jesus on a regular basis, He's given us a really big hint as to where He hangs out (see Matthew 25:40).

We need Jesus to teach us how to fight like He did. The war is over but the battles rage daily as we encounter enclaves of the enemy. There are still systems we come across that were put on auto-pilot, and they continue to steal, kill and destroy. The dragon is "filled with fury, because he knows that his time is short," and he has determined "to make war against [us]—those who obey God's commandments and hold to the testimony of Jesus" (Revelation12:12,17). We want it to be said of us that we "overcame him by the blood of the Lamb and by the word of their testimony" and that we did not love our "lives so much as to shrink from death" (Revelation 12:11).

Our Pledge

Jesus began the unraveling process and calls us to follow in His steps. This means we must live in such a way that we grab the cut strings on the tapestry woven by injustice and pull it apart. But we don't want to throw away the threads; rather, by his grace, we desire to see them used in new, everlasting patterns in Christ's kingdom. Our desire is to fight like Jesus and wield love in His name.

This requires a pledge of the heart to . . .

. . . love sincerely, hating what is evil, clinging to what is good.

. . . honor others more than ourselves.

. . . stoke the fires of our spiritual fervor so that we never tire of being joyful, hopeful and patient in affliction.

. . . be faithful in prayer.

. . . share with anyone whose need God puts us in a position to meet.

. . . never be so proud or conceited that we are not willing to associate with people of low position; rather, we will identify with them, for Christ saw fit to become one with us.

. . . not repay anyone evil for evil.

. . . be careful to do what is right in the eyes of everybody and, by God's grace, live at peace with our neighbors.

. . . never seek revenge or allow evil to overwhelm us; rather, we promise to overcome evil with good.[30]

When we do, we join arms with those who have

---

[30] Paraphrase of the instructions given to believers living in Rome before the persecution (see Romans 12:9 ff).

walked in God's way of winning by losing. Some have suffered unto death and are now in His presence, beneath the altar. Even now, they cry out. There have been so many who have recognized that there is no defense against sacrificial love. Consider those who put evil on display when dogs were turned loose on them, and they did not strike back because they loved the dog and, more so, the one who let go of the leash. Recall when water from fire hoses stung their skin and police beat them with batons, yet they sang in their suffering, "We Shall Overcome." And they did. God did through them. God will through us.

Chapter 7

Cup-Drinking

Submission

It was the middle of the night when Jesus knelt, sweating drops of blood, in an olive press. How ironic. The olive garden known as Gethsemane was not only a place where they grew olive trees, it was also where they harvested and processed the fruit of this symbol of peace. And now, the Prince of Peace, takes His turn. Imagine being there. Walk past the sleeping disciples and kneel silently next to Jesus. It is here that we realize His suffering began earlier than we knew. The mocking, brutality and nails are still to come, but here, in this garden, He is already suffering. Jesus felt squeezed and pressed on as the emotional burden overwhelmingly crushed Him.

That dreadful night in Gethsemane, all Jesus wanted was His friends and His Father. His friends failed—for the flesh is weak 'round midnight—and, at first glance, it appears the Father did too. While Jesus' best friend, John, could not wait an hour with him, he did stay awake long enough to hear Jesus pray, "Father, if it is possible, may this cup be taken from me" (Matthew 26:39).

I'm a dad, and when I see one of my children in pain, I respond to them. That night, however, Jesus' father didn't. Jesus even called, "Daddy." This is the same, intimate way He taught us to talk to God, even though it was considered blasphemous when He said it. He also said, "Which of you fathers, if your son asks for a fish, will give him a snake instead? Or if he asks for an egg, will give him a scorpion? If you then, though you are evil, know how to give good gifts to your children, how much more will your Father in heaven give the Holy Spirit to those who ask him!" (Luke 11:11-13),

I have confirmed this to be so true. I didn't have a daddy until I had God. And I have found that my Father knows me, loves me and meets me in my needs. Our Father provides for me beyond measure, and I know that if I were to cry out to Him for help, He would come running. Still, when Jesus—God's only begotten Son—called out, His cries were met with disheartening silence. All He asked was for the cup to be taken from Him. He didn't want to go to the cross. God, why didn't You respond? Why didn't You send ten thousand angels to bring Your Son home? Why did You risk being seen as a dead-beat dad who is inattentive to Your child's cry?

It has to do with the cup doesn't it?

Not Our Cup of Tea

When Jesus asked God to take the cup, He wasn't just referring to the physical pain of the cross. As bad as the scourging and nails would be, the cup represents something even worse: the wrath of God.

In the Old Testament alone there are at least twenty different words and over five hundred eighty verses that describe the wrath of God. I usually skip over them in favor of the parts of the Bible that speak of God's love, compassion and mercy, but if we are going to fully know God and completely understand the wondrous cross, then we must be willing to face the existence of the cup of God's wrath.

> In the hand of the Lord is a cup full of foaming wine mixed with spices; he pours it out, and all the wicked of the earth drink it down to its very dregs. (Psalm 75:8)

Or:

> Awake, awake! Rise up, O Jerusalem, you
> who have drunk from the hand of the
> Lord the cup of his wrath, you who have
> drained to its dregs the goblet that makes
> men stagger . . . Therefore hear this, you
> afflicted one, made drunk, but not with
> wine. This is what your Sovereign Lord
> says, your God, who defends his people:
> "See, I have taken out of your hand the
> cup that made you stagger; from that cup,
> the goblet of my wrath, you will never
> drink again. (Isaiah 51:17,21-22)

Let us try to understand the anger of God. Our
Father is not capricious and random in His wrath. Try
to imagine what it feels like to have created everything
good, only to see it go bad. In the garden, everything
was perfect. We had perfect union with God and each
other. Freedom was a way of life, and we could even
name the animals. All our Father asked was that we
stay away from one tree. Adam and Eve couldn't, and
we haven't either. Because our cups were full of sin,
God's cup filled with wrath, for that is the only just
response to the genocides we perpetrate, the children

we kill, the hatred we inject, the vulgarity we accept and the innocence we steal. Wrath is the only reasonable result to what we have done to God's good world.

The statement that God acts one way in the Old Testament and another in the New Testament isn't true. Some say God has a split personality—one of wrath and another of love—depending on where in the Bible we look. But the cross negates that assertion. The cross is in the New Testament, and in addition to being about love and forgiveness, it is also the ultimate display of God's justified wrath. Jesus hung on the cross and was brutalized. Why? He did so to make peace, pay a price, achieve victory, absorb our pain AND ALSO because of God's wrath against our sin.

The cross is about propitiation. Theologians say it means, "to satisfy." Christ's work on the cross was not meant to merely appease the Father's wrath but to absolutely satisfy and satiate His righteous burning, once and for all.

What Wondrous Love is This

Who killed Jesus? We point to the Romans soldiers. They were the ones who perfected crucifixion as a form of torture, and they were the ones who actually implemented the death sentence. Or we draw attention to the religious leaders who wrongly convicted Jesus of blasphemy, a conviction that was punishable by death. The introspective among us look in the mirror and say, "I did."

Yet in this discussion about who killed Jesus, we leave out one person: God.

> Surely [Jesus] took up our infirmities and carried our sorrows, *yet we considered him stricken by God, smitten by him*, and afflicted. But he was pierced for our transgressions, he was crushed for our iniquities; the punishment that brought us peace was upon him, and by his wounds we are healed. We all, like sheep, have gone astray, each of us has turned to his own way; and *the Lord has laid on* him the iniquity of us all . . . *Yet it was the Lord's will* to crush him and cause him to suffer. (Isaiah 53:4-6,10a, emphasis added)

The cup contained the wrath of God. "For God so loved the world that he gave [sent, offered up, handed over] his only son" (John 3:16). Now we see why God didn't take the cup from His Son's hand. If He had, His wrath would have remained. It would still need to be satisfied. If the Father responded to Jesus' cries in the garden and removed the cup from Him, then someone else would need to drink. He would have given it to me—to us. But, "For God so loved the world!"

I can't imagine drinking the cup of God's wrath just for my sins alone. What a bitter cup. "Thank you, Jesus. Thank you, God, for leaving the cup in Christ's hands!" How agonizing that must have been. The good news is that Jesus drank the cup in its entirety and fully satisfied the wrath of God.

What wondrous love is this, O my soul, O my soul; What wondrous love is this . . .

Sing, my soul, sing! For you have not tasted the cup. The bitter gall never touched your lips, for Father, Son and Holy Counselor loved us more than we had known. Sing, my soul *what wondrous love is this . . .*

that caused the Lord of Bliss, to bear the dreadful curse for my soul . . .

I admit that I couldn't see past the physical torment. But the meaning of the curse of that tree lies not only in the humiliation but also the "why" beneath the surface. Forgive me for ignoring what Your Scripture so clearly teaches about Your righteous indignation. Forgive me for not telling others. I thought that if I did, I would then have to defend You because they wouldn't comprehend. I now understand . . . and I'm on my face, singing . . .

To God and to the Lamb, who is the great "I Am," While millions join the theme, I will sing, I will sing. While millions join the theme, I will sing.

For I never have to wonder if You are mad at me.

Your Cup

What cup is God offering to you and to me? The death of Jesus is our way of life; therefore, we must drink our cups too. It seems like each of us who would take up our cross must answer this basic question: *Have I surrendered to the life that my Daddy has for me?*

The cup that sits in front of us is not the same cup that was served to Jesus. His was a cup of wrath. Ours contains something different but requires no less of a response.

Christ paved the way when He concluded His request, "Yet not as I will, but as you will" (Mark 14:36). Jesus surrendered to the life chosen for Him. Three times He yielded to Abba's will. For as Ken Gire writes, "…more than He feared the cup, He loves the hand from which it comes".[31]

The Holy Spirit leads each of us to our own private Gethsemanes where we must learn how to surrender to God's will and not ours.[32] In our own gardens, sometimes late at night, God places a cup before us

---

[31] Ken Gire, "Moments with the Savior: A Devotional Life of Christ, (Zondervan: Grand Rapids, 1998) p328
[32] Acknowledgements to William Barclay.

and we wrestle with the pressure. We struggle with surrender and His call.

The content of our cups are different. To the one who desires a wife, God has served the cup of singleness. For another, one who vowed "for better, for worse," the cup offered has more worse than better. To the couple that begs for a child, the cup contains a child, but not the child they wanted. This one cries all night and is sick all of the time.

As excruciating as it can be, we must resign ourselves to our cup. We must cease comparing our contents to our fellow followers. When we do, when we give in to comparison and cast sidelong glances at the lots of others, we hear what Jesus said to Peter when he wanted to know what Jesus' plans were for John: "what is that to you?" (John 20:21ff).

We submit. We surrender to the life God has chosen for us. We drink the cup served to us.

Sometimes we run to God, knowing that He will hold us. He always does, but at times His embrace is more like that of a parent holding a child at the doctor's office as the nurses enter the room to administer a shot. It's confusing because we know our Father loves us, yet He allows the pain and, seemingly, does nothing about it. But it is still Him holding us. We must trust that He will never allow an unneeded tear to come our way, though He will allow tears.

The question is not, "Do we like the cup?" Jesus didn't relish His cup and thus shows us that it is acceptable to ask the Father to take it away. Jesus asked Daddy three times to take it, and three times He submitted to His Father's will. Paul did the same thing with the thorn in his flesh: "Three times I pleaded with the Lord to take it away from me" (2 Corinthians 12:8). But then he surrendered to the life God had for him. The question is not if we want the cup; rather, it is do we love the hand from which it comes? Because if we do, then we can follow in the footsteps of Jesus and drink it with joy.

Choosing the Cross

I have been crucified with Christ.
Galatians 2:20

Chapter 8

Giant Steps

Dedicated

The cross. We wear it. We print it on ball caps. We sing about it.

There are some who say we should give up this fascination with the cross. I agree that we could do with less commercialization of the cross, but that's only one of the issues they raise. They also say that, at a foundational level, the cross itself is a problem. That it too quickly becomes a barrier between Christians and others.

It's certainly true that there are some in this world who hate the cross. Gracia Burnham experienced that hatred firsthand. In the spring of 2001, she and her husband, Martin, were captured by Muslim terrorists and held hostage. After almost a year in captivity, her husband was shot and she was set free to tell the story.

The Burnham's captors possessed an intense hatred for the cross. Robert Webber writes, "One day when the Burnham's were being marched past a Muslim village, they came across a small Christian chapel. One of the rebels said, 'There used to be a cross there, but we destroyed it. We hate the cross. Any time we see a cross we destroy it if we can." Prior to her kidnapping, Burnham says that she was not "a real cross fan. I was raised a Baptist, and [the cross] always seemed Catholic to me. But I love the cross since my captivity; and I have it everywhere."

If I could have my way, the cross would be everywhere as well. I'm not talking about insuring that all churches have a physical cross in the sanctuary or on top of their steeple. I don't even mean that I would like to see more cross sculptures or representations in peoples' houses. Rather, as Christians are everywhere, the cross should be everywhere—because we live it. But this requires a giant step.

My friend, Stace Tafoya, is an Episcopal priest. His ordination was uplifting, sobering and a great example of this giant step. During the service he committed to a life of love and service, a life dedicated to caring for young and old, strong and weak. He would proclaim God's forgiveness for sinners and pronounce His blessings for believers.

The presiding Bishop asked him eight questions:

Do you believe that you are called?

Do you commit yourself to this calling?

Will you receive pastoral guidance, even as you give it?

Will you minister the word of God and the sacraments of the new covenant so that the reconciling love of Christ may be known and received?

Will you be a faithful shepherd as you co-labor with the sheep to build the family of God?

Will you pattern your life and that of your family according to the teachings of Jesus?

Will you persevere in prayer publicly and privately?

Stace said "Yes" to all of these vows, and the Bishop blessed him. But my friend will be the first to tell you that what he did does not make him special. Yes, today he wears clerical garments and people call him Father, but he says he is simply a walking symbol for what all Christians are called to be. His black clothing represents that he has died to self. The collar stands for the yoke of Christ. When people look at him and the vows he has affirmed, they now have an image for *themselves*. Stace is what they should be. After all, we are *all* called to be priests of the most high God.

As John writes in Revelation, "to him who loves us and has freed us from our sins by his blood, and has made us to be a kingdom of priests to serve his God and Father" (Revelation 1:5b-6a).

A Christian is one who is called to a life of service. Sometimes, however, we need to "see" before we can "be." We need examples to pattern our lives after. These can come in the form of clergy or a godly grandmother. Someone whom, after we watch his or her life, helps us understand what It looks like. This was key to the Apostle Paul's ministry. He wasn't being arrogant when he said, "Follow my example, as I follow the example of Christ" (1 Corinthians 11:1). No, he was recognizing how spiritual development happens. Paul was about following the example of Christ—that is, following the cross. All of his life was about pain-absorbing, price-paying, peace-making, winning by losing and cup-drinking. He then held this up as a pattern to those who followed him. Eventually Paul was able to step out of the way, and those following in the path would realize that the indentations in the ground were not made by Paul but by Jesus. Peter affirms this when he writes to all believers, saying, "To this you were called, because Christ suffered for you, leaving you an example, that you should follow in his steps"—in his giant steps (1 Peter 2:21).

It is hard to imagine jazz—and even music in general—without the influence of John Coltrane. Any saxophonist wants to follow in his steps, for he invented a new approach to improvisation in which he played scales at a high rate of speed and in rapid succession. "Sheets of Sounds" was the term coined to describe the sensation of the hundreds of notes flowing over his listeners' eardrums. One of the best examples of this is Coltrane's composition called "Giant Steps." Playing this Coltrane masterpiece has become a rite of passage for young saxophonists. After one has learned their instrument and spent much time practicing, there comes the moment when he has to give "Giant Steps" a shot. When a Christian realizes that Jesus, in His death, was showing us how to live, it's almost like a second conversion that requires we count the cost of such a step of faith.

Cross Tattoos

Back to the story of my friend Stace's ordination. What I remember most about the events of that day was when he laid on his stomach, face to the ground and arms stretched out to the side in the form of a cross. The symbolism was clear: Stace was choosing to live as a cross.

Early Christians understood that this choice was not reserved just for clerics and religious professionals.

When they converted to Christianity, they were clear that they were choosing to follow in the ways of the cross. They would stand before their fellow believers and renounce the works of the evil one and the ways of the world. "Then the minister traced the sign of the cross on the head of the new convert proclaiming, 'This is your invisible tattoo, and you now belong to Jesus.'"

To say we belong to Jesus is to release our own claim to our lives and our bodies. We have renounced personal ambition and desires for we "were bought at a price" (1 Corinthians 6:20). The highest price. Christians, that is "little Christ's" or "Christ-like ones," offer ourselves "as living sacrifices" (Romans 12:1), for we have chosen the way of Jesus, which is the way of the cross. "We have been crucified with Christ," and we can say, "I no longer live, but Christ lives in me" (Galatians 2:20).

Dead and Dying

What does this mean? How can we be "crucified with Christ"? Practically, it means that we are dead, yet dying. Death by crucifixion was a long, slow and excruciatingly painful process; the average victim could survive for days. Death usually came in one of two ways: suffocation or starvation. After they were fastened to the cross with ropes or nails, the worst part was yet to come. Breathing became extremely difficult; humans can't breathe when hung by their arms because this position doesn't allow the diaphragm muscle to properly contract. On the cross, each breath required the victim to stand up on the nail in their feet and so relieve tension on the diaphragm. Then they would sag back down, relieving the pain on their feet, transferring it to their arms, wrists and hands. Death would ensue when the person no longer had the strength to stand.

The Romans thought this produced too quick of a death, so they would often fasten a seat on the cross. This allowed the person to rest their legs, but it prolonged their death. Ultimately, if there were no intervention, the person would starve to death.

Understanding what death on a cross looked like, what does it mean for us to be crucified with Christ? It means we must "put to death the misdeeds of the body" so that the flesh no longer holds sway over our lives. Only the Spirit (see Romans 7 and 8).

If we accept the invitation to an excruciating life, it won't be easy. Jesus told us that the call to follow Him is a decision we have to make anew every day. "If anyone would come after me, he must deny himself and take up his cross daily and follow me. For whoever wants to save his life will lose it, but whoever loses his life for me will save it. What good is it for a

111

man to gain the whole world and lose or forfeit his very self?" (Luke 9:23-25).

We must be prepared for others to not understand and to try and distract us. Their appeals will sound so attractive compared to life on the cross. When Jesus was on the cross, there were many people who called Him to come down. They said, "Save yourself! Come down from the cross, if you are the Son of God," and "He saved others; let him save himself if he is the Christ, the Chosen One" (Matthew 27:40 and Luke 23:35). So too we will often face the call from friends and even fellow believers. We, like Jesus, will have the power to do exactly what they are asking, but—for the sake of the world—we must remain.

Our childhood vow of, "Cross my heart and hope to die," becomes a reality when we accept Christ's invitation to follow Him. Oh, but Jesus said that death is life in the kingdom. It is like a seed that falls to the ground and now produces many seeds (see John 12:24). May we, too, fall to the ground, giving way to the growth of spiritual trees and strange fruit that nourishes a world hungry for life—life that comes only from Christ.

The cross isn't all the Christian life is about. Life with Jesus is about worship. Not just what we do on Sundays, but worship as a way of life. It's about the indwelling of the Spirit of God so that we are empowered to serve. It's about staying connected to the vine through prayer so that we have life and nourishment. It's about grace received and grace bestowed. It's about the Kingdom of God that we seek, enter and receive. It's about the resurrection! Jesus sat up in that tomb and the angels rolled the stone away, not so that Christ could get out (He could have walked right through the walls,) but so that *we* could see in. So that we could see that He is risen.

He is risen, indeed!

We as Christians blend all of these aspects, all of these features of our faith, into our daily lives. When we do so, they are like the notes that come together to form chords. With each moment, we compose with life and lips the story of our great God. That composition gains depth and richness when we are sure to include the blue note as well—the blue note of the cross.

The cross is a love supreme. It is *the* pattern and symbol of sacrifice and service. And I believe it is people of the cross that give the church magnetism. Many people are repelled by the church, especially those who feel inadequate or sinful. They avoid the church for fear of judgment and condemnation. The kinds of people that avoid the church today were the kinds of people that were drawn to Jesus. In Christ they found a love supreme. Jesus said, "But I, when I am lifted up from the earth, will draw all men to myself" (John 12:32). Even as Christ hung on the cross, the thief who cursed Him was drawn to Him.

The cross, when lived in the presence of those who are desperate for God, doesn't repel; rather, it attracts like a magnet. So it is with people of the cross. As we humbly follow in the steps of our Lord, the blue note in our lives captures and draws those full of pain. In us they can see relief; they can find a pain-absorbing person. The guilty juvenile offender in need of the mercy that comes only from a price-paying disciple. The arguing couple in need of a peace-maker. Those who have been turned off by religion because all they have seen is arrogance and pomp are longing for the cup-drinking person who is so surrendered that she is willing to lose. Following in the ways of a love supreme attracts those dying to be loved.

Jesus' death on the cross was a supreme act of love. "Greater love has no one than this, that he lay down his life for his friends" (John 15:13). The cross of Christ was a love supreme. People of the cross have the potential to restore the Church's reputation to that of the greater love that marked Jesus' life on earth. This will require that we reject the rugged individualism of our culture in favor of the old rugged cross. But following in the footsteps of our Crucified Christ doesn't have to be a dirge.

The Second Line

A Jazz funeral is a public event. Once a family has memorialized their loved one, they take to the streets. Often the casket is placed in a carriage and family, friends and a brass band march alongside as they make their way to the cemetery. At this point the band is playing somber versions of songs like, "Just a Closer Walk with Thee."

As the "Main Line" of family, friends and the band march home, the atmosphere and tempo changes drastically. The band swings with songs like, "O When the Saints Go Marching In." Handkerchiefs wave, colorful umbrellas twirl and people dance their way through the streets.

Music and the mood are so infectious that a "Second Line" of people form and join in the festivities. Folklorist Nick Spitzer calls the Second Line a "funeral without the body."[33] As Christians, we are the Second Line.

Arthur Blessitt has carried a cross for four decades—literally! In the sixties he was known as the "Minister of Sunset Strip," as he sought to reach drug addicts, prostitutes and Hell's Angels in Hollywood,

---

[33] Nick Spitzer, "Love and Death at Second Line," Southern Spaces, accessed May 14, 2014,
http://southernspaces.org/2004/love-and-death-second-line.

California. One day he sensed that the Lord was leading him to take a cross off of the wall and carry it from Los Angeles to Washington D.C. This would be no easy task with a cross that was twelve feet tall, six feet wide and weighed forty-five pounds. Out of obedience he began his journey Christmas morning 1969.

After walking across the United States of America, he set his sights on the world. One step at a time he walked through every country on every continent: Three hundred fifteen countries, island groups, territories and Antarctica as well. Along the way he went through war and was arrested twenty-four times. Arthur holds the Guinness World Record for the "World's Longest Walk": 38,102 miles. And every step he carried the cross![34]

There is a wonderful documentary about his journeys called, *The Cross: 38,102 Miles. 38 Years. One Mission.* In the movie, you see that as Arthur carried the cross, people were drawn to him, and little children followed as he gave them brightly colored stickers that told them about God's love.

I saw Arthur Blessitt on TV when I was a child, and I've been intrigued by him ever since. As I grew older, I dismissed him as some crazy guy on a crazy mission.

---

[34] Arthur Blessitt, *Give Me a J,* (Legacy Publishers International)

But I've now come to deeply admire him. His love for people is truly amazing. He once said, "Let your vision be no bigger than the next person you meet." His mission was not to walk around the world; his mission was—and is—people.

When I look at what Arthur Blessitt has done with his life, I see—in vivid Technicolor—what Jesus has called all of us to see: His cross is our life.

About the Author

Robert Gelinas is pastor who deeply desires to see people experience God unfathomable love. Especially the poor, the down and out, the disenfranchised and disabled and those deemed unimportant. As he says, "God loves all people and desires them to experience his peace. God also has a special heart for the poor and poor in spirit, the miserable and marginalized."

He leads Colorado Community Church, a multicultural, inter-denominational community of over 3,000 followers of Christ in Aurora, Colorado. He holds a BA in Biblical Studies and an MA in Missiology.

Robert is also an adoption advocate and jazz theologian.

He and his wife, Barbara live with their six children in the Denver area.

For more information please visit: www.robertgelinas.net.

The following is the first chapter of Robert
Gelinas's

Finding the Groove
Composing a Jazz-Shaped Faith

—1—

Setting the Stage

When I was in college, I used to study for my Greek and Hebrew exams at a local jazz venue. I was fascinated as the ensemble played together, in concert with and for each other. As I watched the way the musicians supported one another, casting glances to communicate, and how each instrument complemented its neighbor — IT began to dawn on me.

One time, young and old, rich and poor, country and hip-hop, black, brown, and white, surrounded me. The band had a Latin saxophonist and a young dreadlocked brother on stand-up bass. On piano and drums two middle-aged men, one black and the other white, played together.

As the groove began, the ,saxophone player motioned for someone in the crowd, an elderly black man, who slowly made his way to the stage. His voice was far from perfect, but as this man sang about love gained and love lost . . .

IT was present

he had IT

we wept because of IT

For almost two decades now, I have wondered what it is about this thing called jazz that brings so many kinds of people together. Oftentimes I listen to a saxophonist solo, and I can't help but think that there's something in this for me. When I see an eclectic ensemble allowing for fresh takes on old standards, or as I look around the sometimes smoke-filled room and see that I am sitting with all hues of skin, I sense that there is something in this for the body of Christ.

As followers of Christ I think that we have something to learn from jazz. For as I watch the way Jesus interacted with people, healing one blind man with a word and using saliva on another, I see him improvising. As I ponder how he taught, drawing on old themes in fresh ways, I see IT in Jesus. I see Jesus in IT.

* * *

A jazz-shaped faith is worth pursuing because it balances freedom with boundaries, the individual with the group, and traditions with the pursuit of what might be. I have discovered in jazz a way of thinking, living, communicating — a way of being . . . a groove. Not a rut, but rather a set of factors that converge, creating a place to settle in and space to be.

Jazz is not the solution to all of the flaws of our faith. Rather it is a way for you and me to experience the gospel — the coming of the kingdom of God — in spite of and because of our deficiencies. The revolutionary movement of Jesus crosses racial, cultural, socioeconomic, denominational, and generational divides, and in the midst of our "franchise" approach to life and faith there is a crying need for something old and new, fresh and yet not novel — something that allows for our weaknesses and strengths. A groove that gives new life to the Scriptures, church, and the way we view community. I often wonder what it would look like if we composed a jazz-shaped Christianity.

What if there was a way for Christians to live with the tensions of our faith and to embrace their beauty?

What if you and I experienced church like a jazz ensemble (listening to the beat of the image of God in each of us) and community meant that you and I felt connected, not only to those we can see, but also with those who *have followed* (in past generations) and *have yet* (in future generations) *to follow* Jesus?

What if there is another way to know the Scriptures? What if we experienced the word of God as a song that sets us free to compose, a melody that has room for our voice to join in with the ancients?

What if every moment of life with Jesus is pregnant with promise, containing the potential to be a one-of-a-kind masterpiece?

What if so much of what has gone wrong with America has also produced something that is right and good, allowing for us to live and love with soul because we understand why caged birds sing?

What if we could find the groove and in the process live in IT?

These are the questions I have been asking in the hope of composing a jazz-shaped faith that will lead me closer to the kingdom of God in our midst.

Something Is Out of Sync

This whole issue is personal for me. At times my faith gets out of sync. I have moments when the Scriptures fail to intrigue or inspire. Times when I long for the desire of the psalmist to meditate on them day and night, for them to be food for my soul, for the word to be alive, piercing, and real. At times, it feels as if something is missing. I have an unshakable sense that something is off in the way we pray, read our Bibles, and worship. The barriers of race, class, generation, and denomination continue to keep us apart, and we are not sure of the last time we felt that those in the pew next to us were truly brothers and sisters, let alone those who attend other churches.

I love the church. I believe in it so much that I have given my life to it, but my eyes are wide open: "No institution has accomplished so much for good in this world; none has fallen so short of its calling!"[1] We have to come to grips with the paradoxical truth that "eleven o'clock Sunday may be the most segregated hour of the week as far as any particular parish goes, but it is the most integrated hour of the week as far as the kingdom goes."[2] Something is out of sync. Do you sense it? Do you feel the wobble in the wheel? How can it be that we are alive during one of the greatest moves of the Holy Spirit in history and yet most of us don't even know? We marvel as we read that three thousand people came into the kingdom in Acts 2, yet many estimate that around the world today, some three thousand people *an hour* are coming to know this Jesus whom we serve! Just not here in America.[3]

My undergraduate degree is in biblical studies, and

at seminary I focused on missiology (the study of the mission of the church). My first degree was concerned with what the Scriptures say; the latter focused on how we communicate and live the faith in the various cultures of the world. I never felt called to go to "the mission field" but rather to live in my own country, among my own people, with "missionary eyes."

Contextualization is the process of taking the truths of Christianity in one hand and a given culture in the other, and then discerning what is compatible with the gospel and what needs redemption. For example, is drinking wine, wearing pants, or the practice of some tribes to initiate their boys into manhood by sending them on a lion hunt in line with the ways of Jesus? Many a missionary has struggled with this process because we are not neutral, unbiased observers. We bring our own culture to the faith and often end up trying to make people over in our image. However, there are "eureka moments" when one realizes that something exists in a culture that gives unique form to how the faith can be understood and lived out. Like when Paul was in Athens.[4]

As the apostle walked the streets, he searched for a place of connection. He wondered how to explain the good news to these erudite philosophical people. He was Jewish, but the Athenians were Greek. He could have taught them to be Jewish first and then to follow

Jesus, but God does not require that we shed our culture to know him. Therefore, Paul looked to see if there was something in their culture that would provide a starting point. He happened upon an altar ascribed to an "unknown God." This altar was unique to them, and Paul brilliantly utilized it as a means to deliver the gospel of the kingdom. This altar was not a Christian image, but it could be redeemed for Christ and his purposes.

What if we do what Paul did? What if we do the work of a missionary right here in our own backyard? When I look at our history and culture with "missionary eyes," I see something indigenous that *we have yet to fully explore and apply to our faith*. Embedded in our way of life is something that has shown the ability to produce creativity, diversity, community, innovation, and depth. Moreover, it originated in the church, though the church abandoned it, rejected it, and has all but forgotten that it exists. What is it? It's jazz.

Discovering it caused me to rethink my beliefs. Not what I believe but how I believe what I believe. Seeking an understanding of jazz

> Jazz music celebrates life—human life. The range of it. The absurdity of it. The ignorance of it. The greatness of it. The intelligence of it. The sexuality of it. The profundity of it.
> **Wynton Marsalis, jazz musician**

has led me to experience our mysterious God and the community to which he calls us in ways that have surprised me. Jazz has given me a new desire to truly know God's word and Christ's incarnation, life, death, and resurrection. A jazz-shaped faith has even led me to strive to embrace suffering for all it has to offer and to refuse to waste temptation. It has changed the way I see people, or shall I say, I have begun to not just see people but to hear them and the song of God in their lives.

Before all of that, though, I needed to understand what it was. Those late-night questions, with college books in my hands and a jazz ensemble grooving in the background, set the stage for my journey of composition. What I discovered is that Ralph Ellison was on to something when he said that all of American life is "jazz shaped." By that, he meant that jazz is *more* than music, and therein lies the hope of a composed and composing life with God — culminating in a jazz-shaped faith.

Made in the USA
Las Vegas, NV
04 June 2024

90737957R00083